MW01107172

Relic Hunter
the book

by Ed Fedory

Published by White's Electronics, Inc.
Sweet Home, Oregon

Editor: Mary Hand

Acknowledgements

As with any book, I suppose, a page of this nature is always left for the last writing task. The sentences have been hammered into paragraphs, and those paragraphs have been forged into chapters and fused between two covers. The coals of the furnace begin to cool and the smith wipes his brow, lays down the heavy hammer against the anvil, and looks at the final product. He feels his efforts have been worthwhile and the product will give good and long service to any who should possibly use it...but, in his thoughts he knows that had the metal not been heated properly and pliable, had he selected a hammer of less weight, had his arm not been tested on the anvil on numerous occasions, had someone not taken him aside to teach him his craft, the results might not be half as satisfying. The writer is a smith, and while his raw material and stock are words, instead of iron, few can deny the outside influences that have helped him along the way, and they must be acknowledged.

Donna, my wife, and Evita, my daughter...for their patience and understanding on which I always depend, and usually tax.

Edward and Anna, my parents, who have guided me along the path to becoming a man and gave me the love of the past and the outdoors.

My grandparents, immigrants all, whose adventurous spirits and strong backs helped secure a foothold for me on these golden shores.

The men with whom I have relic hunted, for their support and friendship..their easy laughter and shared experiences in the field.

Rosemary Anderson, editor of Western and Eastern Treasures, for her graciousness and support over the years.

People's Publishing Company for permission to use previously published material appearing in Western & Eastern Treasures Magazine.

Alan Holcombe, of Whites Electronics, for helping make one of my long-held dreams come true.

...and finally...

Jerry Bass, my good friend and mentor, for his sage advice, his tolerance and humor, and his guidance and goodwill over the years of our friendship.

Cover Photo By:
Vincent Arrigali

ISBN 1-882279-02-6

Published by White's Electronics, Inc.
Sweet Home, Oregon

Relic Hunter
the book

Table of Contents

Introduction

Relic hunting opens up an entire new world to those who are quickly becoming bored with following in the wake of other treasure hunters who have stalked those same schoolyards and parks. Intellectually stimulating and physically demanding, relic hunting fulfills the need and desire of those faced with the commonplace tedium that often plagues our daily lives. Instead of simply reading about adventures, it gives an opportunity for the individual to become an adventurer...rather than enjoying a good mystery story, you become the detective with your own mysteries to solve. History, in most cases, gives us only scant clues to the sites of happenings in the distant past, and it is the job of the relic hunter, through minor footnotes, inconclusive paragraphs, old and faded maps, hints and gut instinct, to sift through the shadowy information and find a particular site.

In his attempts to push aside the dark curtains of time and catch a glimpse of the past, the relic hunter must put in long hours and pay some hefty dues along the route of his quest. He must be willing to spend long hours amidst dusty books as well as long hours in the field; deal with librarians and archivists with the same respect and equanimity he uses with farmers and property owners. The relic hunter must be able to smile at his own failures as well as his successes, and amid the swarms of mosquitoes and other inhabitants of the deep woods, be able to grit his teeth, keep spirit, and push ahead with a determined gait to fulfill his mission of recovering bits of history.

Anyone reading the previous paragraphs may well ask themselves the question, "Why bother?" It is not an easy question to answer. In order to do so, I would have to isolate and distill the essential ingredients of hundreds of relic hunts. Perhaps it is the thrill of holding a small bit of the past, say a musketball, that was fired by a British soldier in the defense of his king and country...perhaps it is unraveling the small threads and knots of fact and proving that you can find an encampment that was temporarily used two hundred years ago...perhaps it is the fellow relic hunters with whom I have searched and shared campfires with over the years as we sought our common dreams in the depths of the soil...and perhaps...just perhaps, it was a slowly evolving passion that could not be denied.

Bringing a group of relic hunting "rookies" into the field is always an interesting experience..especially when recoveries are being frequently made!

Few of us started out as relic hunters. Most started as coinshooters and followed along the path toward relic hunting as we sought those older and still older coins. As we broke century barrier after century barrier, we slowly saw the curtains pushed aside and we wanted to know more about the past. In learning more about the periods of time forming our history, we may have seen that some of the things we had collected in our "junk" boxes were not trash, but significant finds relating to our country's past...and the more we learned, the more we wanted to know. Looking back on it now, after decades, it seemed like such a natural progression—much like a cork in a stream, bouncing from rock to rock, experience to experience, until finally coming to rest in a pleasant and tranquil pool.

One of the real joys I have had over my years of relic hunting has to be the introduction of this facet of our hobby to other detectorists. Witnessing, as I have, the marvel of a "rookie" holding his first musketball from the American Revolution, or being there to watch as that first trade ax is recovered after having been lost for over two centuries, is an incredible experience. I have seen people who hadn't read a history book since high school suddenly standing beside me in the library as they sought to know more about local or national history, as a result of their first relic hunting experience. I have been privileged to witness the awe expressed on elementary school children's faces as I rolled a recently recovered cannonball across the classroom floor, and knew that seeing that relic gave them a greater understanding of what their social studies textbooks could only attempt to give in the form of pictures.

The purpose of this book is as a "primer" of sorts for those coinshooters and detectorists who would fancy a little more adventure in their hunts as well as their lives. In that sense, I hope to provide you with a few short-cuts and hints on how to make your initial experiences as relic hunters a successful endeavor. I would also be remiss if I didn't add that another purpose of this book is to display and illustrate some of the skills needed to preserve and understand our past as a nation, as far too often, when viewed by the archaeological community, our efforts and pursuits are seen in the poorest and weakest of lights.

Relic hunters with their passion and efforts provide an essential link in our knowledge of the past that is too often overlooked...none of us profess to be infallible experts in the field of relic hunting, only older and humble students of our nation's history and the skills we have acquired which enable us to achieve a greater understanding of our past.

To all those "older students" and the men with whom I have hunted, this book is dedicated.

- EAF

Chapter 1

Your Detector

Most detectors in the marketplace today will serve adequately when it comes to the needs of a relic hunter, but that is not to say that all will serve equally as well.

Knowing your detector, and knowing it WELL, is an essential. If you are just beginning to detect, it is imperative that you log some hours with your detector in the field. You can't just assemble your detector, and plan on meeting with success the first day out. Read the manual that comes with your detector, and upon completing it, take your detector and manual to the nearest schoolyard and begin learning, step-by-step, how it works.

Having used many different brands and models of detectors over the years, I still like to search a schoolyard when I am beginning to learn how a new model detector works. Attempting to understand your new detector while in a tangle of brush or in a stalk stubbled cornfield can prove to be a highly frustrating experience.

If you are an experienced coinshooter, and understand your detector well, you can consider some of your dues already paid. Relic hunting, however, is an entirely different game from coinshooting, in that many targets that you wouldn't have even given a second thought about digging in a park or on a ball field will become a desired target.

Discrimination

On a metered detector, a target falling in the foil or pulltab range may, in many cases, prove to be a musketball or a colonial pewter button. With relic hunting, finding a coin of the period is

New metal detecting technologies coupled with increased depth and target ID are making deeper and significant relic recoveries possible.

the exception rather than the rule. Generally, your most common find will be lead projectiles, either dropped or fired, and you should know where these objects can be found on your meter. Ground conditions and the size of the projectile may also affect how your detector's meter will read on the object and you should be aware of this fact. It might be helpful for the beginning relic hunter to check out his detector on small split-shot or a small lead sinker to determine where the individual detector will register.

The new wave of high-tech detectors offers the relic hunter the ability to gather all types of information about the target before it is dug. Tone ID accompanied by graphic displays of the target is especially helpful when working in a very trashy area such as is often found when relic hunting the sites of old forts and blockhouses. Questionable signals are often reduced in number when more information is available and as a result, less time is spent digging poor targets.

On detectors without meters, the relic hunter must know where each of the desired metals will drop off or be discriminated out of the range of detection. A discrimination setting which is too high will cause you to miss quite a number of desired relics. Find an opportunity to check your detector against small pewter or brass buttons, and be sure that your detector is accepting them with solid target signals. Buttons, especially those which are regimentally marked, are among the most desirable objects relic hunters seek. Marked or numbered buttons will verify troop encampments or positions during a battle or skirmish and can easily be traced through history. The knowledge obtained from one simple button can be invaluable for future hunts...especially when new strategies are being developed. Be doubly sure these are acceptable targets to your detector.

When working in the field during a relic hunt, use the lowest possible discrimination level possible. This will vary according to the particular type of situation in which you find yourself. If you are seeking the site of a temporary encampment, you may choose to search in the ALL METAL mode on your detector, as targets will be few and far between. On the other hand, if you are searching the site of a stockaded fort where tons of nails were used during its construction, working in an all metal mode can prove to be one of life's most frustrating experiences! Under such conditions, a discrimination setting that rejects most of your small iron targets is desired. Eliminating small iron fragments will still allow your detector to pick up larger iron targets such as cannonballs, mortar bomb fragments, or belt axes. If a target is questionable, it should ALWAYS be dug.

Sensitivity

All mid and top of the line detectors have adjustments for the sensitivity of the detector. The higher the sensitivity is set on the detector generally equates with the depth at which targets will be detected. How high you will be able to set your detector's sensitivity will be determined by the site you are working. In a situation where you are encountering large amounts of fragmentary iron, you may want to back off on your sensitivity or increase the amount of discrimination on your detector. This balance between sensitivity and discrimination I often refer to as "threading the needle". Being able to run your sensitivity to near max and your discrimination near minimum, is an ideal relic hunting situation...unfortunately, we don't always find ourselves on IDEAL sites, and a compromise must often be made. A good, general rule of thumb is to run your sensitivity as high as your detector and ground conditions will allow while still being stable.

Coil Size

Most detectors are shipped from the manufacturer with a standard mid-sized coil, which is generally seven to eight inches in diameter. This size coil is ideal for coinshooting, but has its limitations when relic hunting, especially on a site that has been "hammered" on numerous previous occasions by other relic hunters. The seven inch coil has only a few advantages under relic hunting conditions—it can get into some tight areas which may prove to be difficult with a larger coil—because of its smaller diameter, it can easily wheedle through ground that is laden with small iron fragments—and finally, pinpointing your individual targets will be much easier. The major disadvantage of the standard coil is its DEPTH, and to a relic hunter this is a primary concern.

Most detectors have a variety of optional coils to meet specific needs and ground conditions encountered in the field.

The majority of metal detector manufacturers offer an optional larger coil for their models. It is advisable to purchase one of these coils, as you will probably find that it will be your first choice on most sites. The added depth will more than make up for the difficulty in pinpointing targets. If the additional weight proves to be too cumbersome or uncomfortable, you always have the option of hip-mounting your detector. Initially, you may find that using a large coil feels like you have a garbage can lid attached to your lower pole assembly, but you will quickly get used to it. By the same token, once you have become familiar and comfortable using the large coil, using a standard coil will feel like you are pushing a bottle cap across the ground with a stick.

Since relic hunting is often not only a test of physical endurance, but of equipment durability, I always suggest the use of coil covers. I wish I had a nickel for every nick and deep groove I put into some of my coils before I started using protective covers. While your mind is wandering on what the site may have once been like, and dwelling on where troops may have moved, the sharpened edge of a rock will often go unnoticed as it protrudes just above the forest floor. Coils are expensive and coils covers are cheap...the logic is sound.

By way of summary, go for the larger coil, and it will increase for chances of success in the field. Remember, some of the relics we are searching for have been buried in the ground for over two hundred years...and they are DEEP!

Factory Pre-Sets and Options

Some detector brands offer factory pre-set programs. These programs offer the novice an easy way to meet with initial successes when using a new detector. As the user becomes more proficient with his detector, he may desire to use his own specially designed program, an "enchancement" program, to fine tune the detector to the type of metallic arifacts for which he is searching. Some detectors offer a wide variety of options from which the detectorist can choose to custom detail a pathway to field successes. Saving such a program in the memory of a detector will allow the relic hunter to "access and go" as soon as his boots hit the field

Remember, no matter what brand or model of detector you have, some successes will be encountered in the field as long as you understand how your detector works. It is the "man behind the machine" that determines success or failure during a relic hunt and there is no substitute for experience.

Digging Tools and Equipment

Obviously, your metal detector is your primary tool for finding relics, but finding them, and being able to recover them are two different stories. Since most of the relics you target will be deep, it is necessary that you have strong and durable tools to aid you in the recovery. Additionally, the relic hunter often finds himself in the deep woods and brush where not only is the depth of your target going to be a problem, but ROOTS as well. Being able to reach your target with ease will be impossible if not for the proper tools.

Using heavy duty digging tools is a MUST when relic hunting. This "nest" of musketballs was recovered under ten inches of brick-hard soil and roots.

There are several criteria for a good relic hunting recovery tool. First of all, the tool must be strong and have good weight, and yet not be too cumbersome or awkward. The digging tool must be sharp and easily handled. It should allow for a certain amount of leverage without being exceptionally long. The tool should also be adaptable for your pack as you hike to the site, and equally adaptable to your belt during the hunt.

I have one recommendation for a tool that meets all of the above criteria...the WILCOX ALL-PRO model 201 digger. This digging tool is fashioned from thick steel, and is coated to be rust resistant. The entire tool is fourteen inches long and both the handle and blade are fabricated from the same piece of steel making the tool virtually indestructible. The handle has a comfortable rubber grip and the length of the tool makes it very easy to lever large rocks from the bottom of your hole. Equipped with a triangular blade at the tip, it cuts through soil with ease, while the sharpened side blade allows you to hack through a web of thick roots on your way to recovering the target. The tool fits comfortably in a sheath, or can be worn, reversed, in a hammer holster.

Another tool that you might want to include on your list of necessary items is the army entrenching tool. This is a small, collapsible shovel that can be of aid when you have to dig deeper on your way to recovering a large target. This tool is not easily adaptable to extended field use as it is awkward when attached to a belt. Bring one along and leave it in your pack...just in case!

The Pack and Its Contents

Having your detector ready and your digging tool at your side, carrying all of your equipment to the site is the next important factor with which to deal. A medium size pack should fill all of your needs. It should be well-made, durable and comfortable. The pack you choose should have plenty of room, as well as outside pockets for your smaller pieces of equipment and finds. The pack I use comes from L.L. Bean, has an integral frame, two side pockets,

and a large back pocket. It is waterproof and has a doubly rein-
forced waterproof bottom. Another pack that meets all the criteria is the army "ALICE" pack.

Depending on where you live in the country, some of the
things you will want to throw into your pack might vary. For
example, we don't have many poisonous snakes in my neck of the
woods, so a snake bite kit is not on our list of priorities, however, it
is a smart move to pack a small first-aid kit. Other things you
might want to include in your pack are back-up batteries, spare
coil, insect repellent/tick spray, headsets, canteen of water, camera,
digging tool, Swiss Army knife, food, portable sterno stove, eating
utensils, flashlight, whistle, compass, maps, etc. Depending on
where you are going, how far you are going, how familiar you are
with the locale in which you are relic hunting, and how long you
plan on staying in the woods, your list and needed equipment will
vary. It is wise to be prepared for the unexpected, but unnecessary
to weigh yourself down with so much equipment that you'll be out
of energy before you reach the site and begin your relic hunt.
Also, in the best case scenario, you should be packing out more
weight when you begin your hike away from the site than when
you were hiking to it. If you are relic hunting with a team or a
partner, which you should be, avoid too much duplication in some
of your equipment. Check your pack before you leave the car or
truck and leave behind all unneeded equipment...it will leave
more room for carrying out all those relics you hope to find!

Clothing For The Field

Once again, the key word is durable, no matter what season
you are relic hunting, it is always wise to have more clothing than
less. You want to be comfortable while you are searching, and
since many of us head out for sites before dawn, the day will
generally get warmer as it progresses. Instead of wearing very
heavy clothing, several layers of lighter clothing is far better. In
this way, as the day gets warmer you can shed layers of clothing

when no longer necessary. This is especially true during the spring and summer seasons. If you are relic hunting in late fall, it might be wise to add an additional hooded sweatshirt to your pack before heading out.

During warmer weather it is fine to wear a short sleeve shirt when working open fields, but whenever you find yourself in the woods or brush, it is advisable to wear a long sleeve cotton shirt. You may work up a sweat, but covering the skin from insects, poisonous plants, thorns, and other associated minor irritations of the woods, is well worth a little discomfort. During the summer months I also avoid wearing jeans, instead, opting for cotton military pants with cargo pockets...the baggier, the better. Let's face it, when you're out in the field, covered with dirt from your eyeballs to your toes, it's not the time to be thinking about making some kind of fashion statement! Also, don't wear short pants on a relic hunt...as bug-bait you'll spend more time swatting than sweeping.

Having checked the weather reports before you set out for your hunt, you'll have a good idea of what to expect in the field. It is advisable to have a rain slicker of some type handy, just in case. Generally, I'll keep my rain gear in the trunk of my car, but if the sky looks ominous before we head for the woods, you'll always find it stuffed into my pack...BE PREPARED.

BOOTS...don't leave home without them. A good pair of leather, ankle high boots is another essential when relic hunting. Whether you are hiking to a site, or using your feet to hold down brush so you can sweep your detector, what you are wearing on your feet is very important. Never wear sneakers during a hunt. On rough terrain sneakers are not equipped or designed to give the necessary support needed by the ankles, nor are the soles generally heavy enough to provide comfort when crossing rocky ground. A pair of old work boots with heavy cotton socks are the "hot ticket" item when it comes to relic hunting in the field.

During the fall and winter it is advisable to wear a knit hat.

Layered clothing and gloves are a necessity when working the fields in early spring or late fall. Remember to always bring a little more clothing than you think you might need.

Most of your body heat will be lost through your head if it is exposed, and a knit hat allows you to continue using your headsets in comfort. During spring and summer hunts a ball cap or sweatband will keep the sweat from running into your eyes as the temperature rises.

*   *   *   *

Well, let's see—you've gotten your detector straightened away, your digging tool is on your hip, your pack is loaded, and with the style of clothing you are wearing, you even LOOK like a relic hunter. So far, you're all decked out and dressed up...WITH NOWHERE TO GO. We'll fix that problem in the next chapter with a little fine-tuning of your research skills!

Chapter 2

Research

Putting yourself and your detector in the right area in which to make a relic recovery will depend on how well you do your research.

Remember, if the coil doesn't go over it, you won't detect it. Research will increase your chances of making numerous and important finds.

Most of us, when in school, hated to do homework...and basically, that's a good word to describe your research. On the other hand, you'll find that once you have gathered some background information on potential sites, searched the site and come home with some interesting finds, that the homework of research is something you will be looking forward to doing, rather than avoiding.

The scope and focus of your research will depend on your areas of major interest and the area of the country in which you reside. Learning more about the town and county in which you live is a good place to begin your research. Most libraries have a section devoted solely to local history...ask the librarian to suggest a good, general book on the area in which you live, and investigate some of the older areas in your neighborhood. You'll be surprised at some of the interesting and important events that happened in your own backyard.

While checking out local events, see how those events fit into the larger puzzle of history on a national level. Broaden your scope to include historic happenings that occurred within a hundred mile radius of where you live. Did any Civil War battles or Revolutionary War skirmishes happen in your area? Where were the crossing points and early bridges along nearby rivers and creeks? Were any military encampments mentioned in your research of the area? Asking yourself questions of this type will help to uncover places you might want to investigate further.

Once you have narrowed your research to a particular event or area, gather as much information as possible. Many libraries are members of an inter-library loan program, and if the books you need are not to be found on the shelves of YOUR library, the book should be able to be retrieved from another library for your use.

When you are in the process of "fine-tuning" your research, get the most primary source of information possible. One way to determine a primary source is to check the bibliography on a more general work and see what books the author used or quoted during the process of writing his own book. If you can find a journal from your period or area of interest, you will find it to be filled with highly specific information. For example, having finished reading a biography of the famous ranger leader, Major Robert Rogers, I checked the bibliography of the book and noticed that the author used a copy of Rogers' original journal as his primary source of information. I made it my mission to find a copy of those journals and recently I was able to obtain a copy. Reading Rogers' own words, thoughts, and observations, first-hand, gave me not only an understanding of the man, but of some of the sites he had frequented. Reading the rules for rangers that he had written almost two hundred and fifty years earlier, gave me ideas of the type of terrain I should search in order to discover some of the encampments used by his ranger forces. The insights into history that can be achieved by reading journals—the fact that a journal puts you right beside the chronicler and observer as he witnessed the events he is reporting, is a tool for the relic hunter that can never be underestimated.

If you live near the capitol of your state, make a point of visiting your state archives. State archives are the repository of thousands of original records, accounts and documents that are invaluable to the serious relic hunter. On each of my visits to our state archive, I am amazed at the amount of solid facts and research with which I am provided in just a few short hours.

On the Federal level, the National Archives in Washington, D. C. can be of invaluable service. When making a request to the National Archives, the request you make should be of a very specific nature. For example, asking for the troop movements in New York State during the period of the American Revolution would encompass far too much information, but asking for a map of West Point during that same period would probably be a request they could easily fill. There will be a cost for photostating, but the research time spent filling your request and tracking down your information is free. Take advantage of this service and you'll see some of your tax dollars well spent. To contact the archives write: NATIONAL ARCHIVES AND RECORD SERVICE, GEN-ERAL SERVICE ADMINISTRATION, WASHINGTON, D.C. 20408.

If you have been among the few fortunate relic hunters who have recovered artifacts bearing the name of a particular soldier, the Federal government might be able to provide you with some information concerning his history in the military. To obtain information on a particular soldier you should write to the REFER-ENCES SERVICE BRANCH, CNNIR NATIONAL ARCHIVES AND RECORD SERVICE, 8TH AND PENNSYLVANIA AV-ENUES NW, WASHINGTON, D.C. 20408. Be sure to request form NATF-#80 (7-84). Be sure to order four copies of the Vet-eran Records form.

Local historical societies are often the repository for interest-ing and useful information. It is a good idea to make a point of joining your local historical society as their publications will often provide you with information on older sites in your community. Town and county historians will often be more than eager to answer any questions you have about your area...seek them out as an invaluable aid to your research.

Being a good listener and observer is important to the relic hunter. On more than one occasion, while listening to deer hunters exchanging tales of the their hunts, I've heard mentions made of a pile of stones in the woods, or the remains of an old colonial home far off the beaten path. Within a half hour I had a crudely drawn map on the back of a napkin and the name of the property owner who had given permission to the hunters to use their land. Armed with this important information I was able to obtain permission to search the site with my metal detector. On one of those sites I was able to pull close to a dozen early large cents, several dating from the late 1700s, while a partner of mine, on a totally different site, found through the efforts of hunters, was able to recover two colonial axe heads and several pieces of gun furniture from a first model Brown Bess musket. Being a good listener and knowing what questions to ask can often lead the relic hunter down the road to making some great recoveries.

Keeping track of your relic hunting information is important. Some method of record keeping should be employed so you have old information readily available and at your fingertips. I like to keep my records, notes, photostats and maps in manila file folders. Each folder is labeled for a specific area or event, and it's an easy process to simply pull out the file drawer to retrieve my research on a particular site or add some newly acquired information which might come in handy on some future hunt.

Maps - An Important Research Tool

Once you have narrowed down the area in which you plan to relic hunt, maps of the area become of significant importance. Several different types of maps will be needed.

The first type of map you will want to have is an old map of the area you plan on searching. Old maps will provide you with a picture of the way the site was long ago. On several old maps I have used in the past, I was able to locate old military roads, encampments, stockaded posts, the original ford of the river, several earthen works and a pair of redoubts which were con-structed at a narrow point in the river to prevent a water approach to the site by an enemy force.

Using that centuries old map in conjunction with a modern topographic map allowed me to achieve several of the individual sites and recover a number of interesting relics. Comparing the bend in the river on both maps gave me an idea of where to begin my search. It also showed me the number of changes which had taken place during those intervening years. The digging of a barge canal destroyed the site of the stockaded post and a housing development was constructed on the site of the encampment.

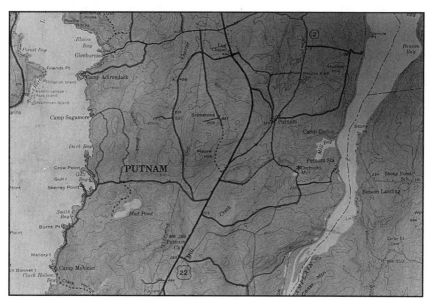

Modern maps of the hunt area used in conjunction with original maps will help the relic hunter place himself "on site" with greater ease. Familiarity with topographic maps is not only a necessary skill for relic hunters, but knowing the lay of the land is essential when attempting to plot troop movements and possible encampment locations.

Don't be too disappointed if even more considerable changes have taken place in the areas you are researching, as the wheels of progress have crushed many sites of the past that would be considered highly significant by today's relic hunters. These are minor setbacks that must be encountered by all relic hunters and often outlying or surrounding sites might still remain untouched ... remember, even a small site can produce a wealth of interesting artifacts and relics.

Check with your state archive and local historical society for copies or photostats of old maps. You might also consider photographing older maps and have enlargements made from which to conduct this portion of your research. Topographic maps are available from the United States Geological Survey offices in your state. To get in touch with your regional offices contact the U. S. Geological Survey, Map Distribution, Federal Center, Building 41, Box 25286, Denver, CO 80225, Phone (303) 236-7477. Your regional offices will send you an index of available maps and an order form for your purchases.

You might also entertain the thought of acquiring an aerial photograph that was used in the production of a particular topographic map. These can be expensive, but often details such as old roads and the remains of foundations can be seen on these high altitude photos with the aid of a magnifying glass.

*　　　　*　　　　*　　　　*

Your research has led you to the site of an early stockaded fort dating from the period of the American Revolution. All of our equipment and packs are in the trunk. The gray light preceding dawn is surrounding us as is the high anticipation of our first relic hunt. You're driving, and I'm your navigator...let's get to the site of that cornfield which hides the remains of the fort and let's see what we can find!

Chapter 3

On Site
The Fine Art of Getting Permission to Search

Locating our site was done with little difficulty...the corn has been harvested and rows of stalk and leaf strewn fields spread out before us for numerous acres, however, finding the site and being able to search the site are two different things. Before attempting our relic hunt, permission from the owner must be granted.

Scanning the horizon, I usually choose the largest and closest farm house in my initial attempts at obtaining permission. Wearing a smile, being pleasant and courteous is the only way of presenting yourself to the owner. I introduce myself, state my desire to search the owner's land, tell something of the general research that has led me to his doorstep, and relate how it is an important site TO ME. I also explain the types of relics or artifacts I hope to recover, how there will be no damage to his land, and how any holes that might be dug will immediately be filled in. I always give the owner as much information as I think he wants to hear. I have gone to the length of taking out my metal detector to show an owner how it works and gone into detailed descriptions as to how a target is dug. In short, you are selling yourself, the hobby, and your historical mission to the owner. I have rarely been turned down when seeking permission to hunt.

There are only a few possible answers the owner can give you in light of your request. If an owner tells me he would rather not let anyone on his field, and offers no explanation as to why, I'm still courteous, I smile, I don't question his decision, apologize for taking up some of his time, and casually mention that I would like to stop by the following year to see if he might have changed his mind.

I have had at least one case where the owner refused permission due to insurance liability. This is not a definite "No" and there are legal ways around the problem. When liability is mentioned, I always counter with offering the owner a notarized affidavit of responsibility. In the affidavit of responsibility, I state that I assume full responsibility for my own safety when on the owner's property and relinquish him from any form of liability for my safety. I then ask the owner if that would solve the insurance liability problem. If permission is still not granted, then we should easily sense that there are other reasons why he does not want us on his land, and we accept his decision.

Nothing pleases a relic hunter more than seeing the ground being turned by the plow on a productive site. Establishing a good relationship with the farmer who owns the property is always desired.

Some farmers rent their fields, and in such cases, it is generally wise to have permission from both parties. If the owner states that he does not want you to search his property because the field is rented to someone else, ask for the other party's name and address and directions to his farm. Continue by asking the owner that if the person to whom he is renting the field grants permission for the relic hunt, would he be agreeable to allowing the hunt to proceed. If the answer is "No" in these types of circumstances, then you have found yourself at a dead end.

Some property owners will be curious to see exactly what it is you have dug up at the end of your hunt. It is a good idea to touch base with the farmer when you are leaving a site. I always like to show the owner some of the things I have found, and explain how some of the relics might have been used in the past. Share some of the information you have recovered through your research with the owner. In some cases he might be totally unaware of the historic events that occurred on his land. He will enjoy hearing about his land and again, it will go a long way toward creating a friendly atmosphere between the relic hunter and the land owner. Establishing a good rapport with the owner is something to be desired...it insures goodwill and will allow you the opportunity to return to the site at a future date.

Sharing information and displaying some of your finds will also show the owner that you have nothing to hide and that you truly appreciate the use of his land. We don't want to give the illusion that we are taking truck loads of gold coins from his fields, or that the smile we wore when we initially asked for permission was a false one.

There is no one who knows his land as well as the farmer, however, there are many things that he might have seen whose significance is unknown to him. To a farmer, the fact that one area of his field contains a large number of stones that he con-stantly drags his plow on, will be considered a mere nuisance, but to the relic hunter it might be seen as evidence of an early homesite or well. Areas where pipe stems or fragments of broken pottery are brought to the surface may certainly be noticed by

31

someone on the seat of a tractor, but these sections of a field will be important areas for the relic hunter to concentrate his search. This sharing of information between the relic hunter and the farmer can be very important and cut down on a good deal of arbitrary ranging about during a hunt on extensive fields.

Getting permission, keeping permission and establishing an above-board relationship with the owner of the property you are searching or attempting to search is the most desirable situation in which the relic hunter can find himself. Take no liberties with the use of the land and astutely avoid any situation that might even remotely suggest that you are taking advantage of the farmer's goodwill. If you desire to bring a couple more searchers into the field with you, check with the farmer beforehand to make sure it is all right with him. Preserve your permission to search the land and your relationship with the owner of the property...it is one of the most important things a relic hunter can do if he expects to continue his search for our country's past!

The Cornfield---The Fort Remains

Having received permission to search the land, the next thing we need to do is "eyeball" it...or do a general visual survey. In this case, we find that the fort is located on the river flats, giving us an opportunity to view it from an elevated area of the roadway that runs parallel to it.

Spread before us we see acre upon acre of corn stubbled rows. What are we looking for...what type of signs can be visible from this distance? Depending on what your research has turned up, you may be able to view the exact site of the fort if you know how to read the ground. Basically, we want to see what elevated areas remain in the field, and note any areas where the field has not been plowed and planted. The latter is the most important feature, in that it usually reflects the existence of a previous structure.

Farmers do not arbitrarily leave small stands of growth in the middle of a field, especially today, without good reason. I have heard it theorized that in the past, a small copse of trees might be left in the field to provide a shady shelter for the farmer when he wanted to take a break from his plowing. It's a nice theory and one that brings a pleasing pastoral image of the past to mind—the plow laying slightly askew, the team of horse idly chomping on the sweet grass at the edge of the trees, the farmer with his back resting against the trunk of a maple, sipping from his wooden rumbler in the shade of the tree. It's a pretty picture...I can feel comfortable with that unstressed image of the past.

In the farming world today, however, where every square foot of field means money in the pocket, leaving a stand of trees is not always economically sound. From the air conditioned enclosure of his tractor, the modern farmer begins to view that stand of trees as an irritation. He can't run straight and true with his plows during the spring and it is an equal irritation during the fall harvest. No, there has to be a reason for those trees having been left in the field and the reason is usually an underlying stone foundation of some size, the stones of which provide a hazard to be avoided by the farmer and his equipment.

As we scan the field from the highway above, we note two small stands of growth, mostly sumac, almost equally distant from the bank of the river and about one hundred fifty feet apart. We know from our research that the size of the fort was about one hundred fifty feet square, and the positioning of the sumacs would coincide with the stone foundations of the blockhouse that occupied each corner of the fort. We decide to pull the car down the farm road for a closer visual inspection of these small stands of trees.

Since we are almost positive that we have located the site of the stockaded fort, we decide to unload our equipment and set up our base camp beneath a large oak on the riverbank. Leaving our detectors with the rest of our equipment, we head to the closest stand of trees. As we make our approach, we note several large cut and dressed foundation stones sticking from the ground at odd angles, and as we near the trees, the incidence of these stones begin to increase. Inspecting the interior of this small "island" of trees, we see where the farmer has thrown several of the larger stones into the tangle of weeds at the base of the trees.

We have found a foundation, but is it the one for which we have been looking? Some method of dating the site has to be established, and this can be done, easily, with some further reading of the ground. There should be pieces of non-metallic evidence lying on the surface that will help us with the dating process.

The first, and usually the most abundant of these clues will be in the form of clay pipe stems. As we walk between the corn rows we easily collect a dozen of these. They are white, cylindrical, pierced with a small hole that runs through its length, and are generally the diameter of a cigarette. When these pipes were molded, the stem sections nearest to the bowl was the largest in diameter and then gradually tapered toward the mouthpiece. The length of the stem, when originally formed, was usually between twelve and eighteen inches long. The fragmented sections found in the field have generally been reduced to a half inch to two inches in length. It is wise to collect and bag all of the pipe stems that you have found in the field, because they can be an invaluable tool for confirming the date of your site.

Another portion of the clay pipes that will be found on the surface of the field, and one that should be collected, as well, are pipe bowl fragments. These will appear as irregularly shaped white fragments with a slight curve. Many of these bowl fragments contain manufacturer's markings and will help us with our dating and understanding of the site. Today, we have collected two bowl fragments that contain markings...one bears an oval cartouche with the imprint of R-TIP-PET, while the second fragment contains the initials RT. In a later chapter, we will see exactly why these two small fragments are significant.

In our search for pipe fragments we have also found several other non-metallic indicators to the age of our site. Several pieces

Washed by the rain and bleached by the sun, a clay pipe stem is clearly visible against the dark soil. Pipe stems are a clear indicator of early activity on the site.

35

of blue and white pottery have been found. On one of the fragments we see the roof of a building of oriental design. Oriental
motifs on plates, cups and bowls were very popular during the
1700s, and we will be sure to collect a large sampling of these, and
other pottery fragments we find while searching the site. The
other type of fragments we have recovered are those made of glass.
One piece is very thick and appears to be black, however, as we
hold it up to the sun we note that it is a very dark green. The
other glass fragment is covered with a thin, iridescent patina that
is easily scratched off, revealing, once again, green glass beneath.
Both of these fragments are common to sites dating from the
1700s and are pieces of rum or wine bottles.

Continuing our search around the small copse of trees, two
other indicators for our site are revealed. At the core of what first
appeared to be a rusty piece of soil, we find the remains of a
rosehead nail, commonly used during colonial times. Our other
evidence is in the form of small bits of red clay, some no larger
than the tip of my small finger. The small red fragments of clay
were once part of bricks that were used to make the chimneys
found in each of the blockhouses. During a report made by a
French ensign who viewed the stockaded fort after it was burned
to the ground, he stated, "all that remained of the fort were twenty
chimneys still standing." From this on-site report, found during
our research, we can expect to find these small red clay fragments
fairly littering the entire site.   Leaving you at the area we have
just examined, I move to the other stand of trees. Each of us is
now positioned on the remains of both of the eastern-most blockhouses. Knowing from our research that we are dealing with a one
hundred fifty foot square, we are determined to locate the two
other blockhouses further out in the field. Walking due west with
the sun at our backs, we begin counting paces. After about fifty
paces, we begin to see evidence of the western-most blockhouses.
Apparently, at some time in the past, the farmer decided it would
be worth his efforts to dispose of the foundation remains. How-

ever, with each plowing more of these stones have worked their way to the surface. Pottery and pipe remains are in evidence, once again.

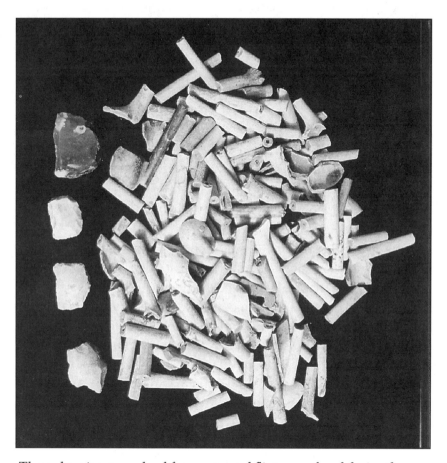

These clay pipe stems, bowl fragments, and flints were found during the course of a two-day hunt on the site of a colonial fort. When such a quantity of non-metallic surface finds are made, we know the ground contains a rich source of metal relics and information.

Assuming that the area with the greatest concentration of stones to be the center of the blockhouse remains, we build a small cairn or pile of stones with the largest and flattest of these so that it is easily visible amid the corn stalks. In this way, it will be easy to see the limits of the fort, as well as the limits of our first day's search of the site.

We have now completed the preliminaries of our relic hunt on the site of this stockaded fort. We have gathered some surface evidence that coincides with our research, we have articulated the area of search between the rock piles and sumac islands, and we are now...almost...ready to begin our relic hunt. The only thing that remains for us to do now is to agree upon a strategy or guideline under which the search will be conducted.

The Strategy of the Hunt

It is of the utmost importance to have a plan or strategy when conducting a relic hunt, especially if you are searching a large structure, as we are here, in the case of our stockaded fort. A systematic and careful approach is desired, so that not only will all of the ground be covered carefully, but that our care with the site will also allow us the ability to document the findings we have made once the search has been completed. This same care should be taken whether you are searching the site of a colonial era home or Civil War hut sites. Being able to document your findings about the site will lead to increasing your knowledge of not only the current site, but of similar sites you may hunt in the future. As relic hunters we are not simply "gatherers and hoarders of relics", as many archaeologists would have people believe, but collectors of information about the past. Our passions for the past are not unlike those of professional archaeologists.

It is counterproductive and a waste of research and time to simply say, "Well, here's our site—LET'S GO!" A haphazard search employing loose patterns and no system will, in the end, lead to a very minimal understanding of the site. You will also not cover all of the ground, resulting in a lot of information and relics being left behind in the soil.

In the case of our fort, covered by the stubble of a harvested

Establishing a systematic strategy for working a site is important so that all areas of a site are covered thoroughly.

crop of corn, a good portion of our strategy has already been dictated to us. Our search patterns have already been established by the rows, making our grid patterns concrete. We will begin our relic hunt by starting our search grids on the east and west sides of the fort about ten rows out from where either the small islands of trees marking the sites of the eastern-most blockhouses and the cairns of stones indicating the positions of the blockhouses on the west are located. To the north and south, our patterns will extend beyond the limits of the fort by a good fifty feet to allow for any artifacts that have been dragged by the plow.

We will begin our search patterns on either side, searching up one corn row and down the next. When significant finds are made, they should be marked. This can simply be done with surrounding stones, or clumps of soil. I usually make a small stack of stones on top of the filled in hole where a recovery was made. In this way, areas of concentrated relics are easily visible as I hunt the field. Later, these relic recovery sites will be added to a rough sketch of the entire site to see if there is some pattern to the types of finds that are being made in a particular area. Having notes on finds, and where they were made, will be important when the site is searched, during the following spring, when the soil has once again been turned over.

With our agreed strategy in place, we move to our respective sides of the site, tune our detectors and begin running a very tight and careful search pattern—we begin the process of gathering information about fort life at an isolated post two centuries ago. Through the recovery of relics we gain in our understanding of the past, and each artifact we collect, each recovery site we mark and document, will allow us to peel back the years and "see" into the past.

Chapter 4

Preserving Your Relic Recoveries

In the late afternoon, we turn our backs on the site, and head to the car. We have spent some time removing the stone cairns we initially set up to mark the positions of the western blockhouses and have made sure there are few, if any, signs that we relic hunted the site.

During the course of the next couple of days this hunt will continue in a different aspect. The recoveries we have made must be cleaned and identified, sorted and labeled. A record of the hunt will be written up and locations of relics mapped. Documentation is an essential if the full story of the fort is ever to be known and shared. Our collecting bags are full, but each recovered relic, if taken individually, offers only a mute testimony to the nature of the site—we are looking for the BIG picture.

Cleaning The Recovered Relics

Great care must be taken with the cleaning of the relics we have recovered. Our biggest fear is that something that has remained in the ground for hundreds of years will be further harmed if we manhandle it. Let's face it, under relic hunting situations, many of the finds we make are fragmentary, especially when we are working on a site that has seen the seasonal effects of the plow. Very few large and intact objects will be found. However, those that have been found, in one piece, should not be reduced to assorted fragments through lack of care.

The cleaning process will depend on the structure and possible delicate nature of the relic as well as the material of which it is composed. The more delicate the item, the greater the care and patience we must exercise during the cleaning process.

Non-metallic Relics

During the course of our relic hunt we have collected an assortment of non-metallic relics. The larger they originally were, the greater the chance that they have been reduced to mere fragments. However, even fragments of a relic—fragments of the story—can offer us information about what life at the fort was once like.

Glass and pottery fragments should be cleaned in lukewarm water with a mild soap to remove soil that might adhere to the surface. A small toothbrush may be used to remove soil, but avoid any excessive scrubbing as the outside veneer on pottery, bearing color and designs, might break free from the clay matrix. Once cleaned of soil, the fragments should be placed on a towel and allowed to dry. Once the pieces are thoroughly dry, they should be placed in a small plastic bag, and labeled. The label should include the name of the site, the period of time from which the site dates, and the date of recovery. If you have recovered many fragments from the same piece of pottery, these should be bagged and labeled separately.

When large quantities of the same pattern are recovered, it is a wise move to see how many of the pieces will fit together. In many cases this will be similar to putting a puzzle together when you don't know either the original shape of the puzzle or the picture that was represented...we also must contend with the additional difficulty factor of not having all the pieces. Long hours and a great deal of patience are needed to try each piece to see if they fit together, but often, the end result of a partially intact piece will be well worth the time and energy expended.

Each time you return to the same site, more fragments of

pottery or glass will be dragged to the surface by the plow, and slowly, over the years, some of the lost pieces to your puzzle will be recovered until the "picture" becomes more apparent. I have one piece of pottery that I have been working on for well over a decade and each plowing allows me to gather at least a couple of new fragments that will hopefully fit into the existing sections. Do I expect this pottery jug dating from the 1750s to ever be one hundred percent intact? Can I realistically hope that I will find every piece that has been distributed over the field during the course of the last two and a half centuries? NO, but each fragment that does fit, allows me a greater view of colonial life.

Musket flints are common non-metallic surface finds on the sites of colonial forts. They are found in various colors, but the most beautiful are the translucent and honey toned.

Pipe fragments should be treated in the same fashion as pottery and glass. The hole in the pipe stems are usually clogged with soil which can easily be removed with a straightened paper clip. All pieces should be carefully examined to see if they bear a

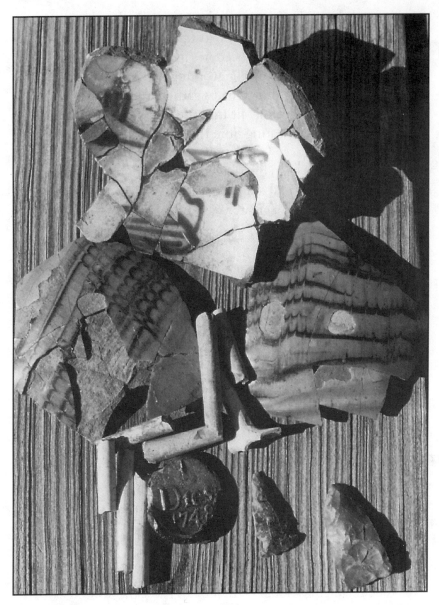

Pottery fragments in association with other non-metallic relics recoverd from the site are good benchmarks in establishing the age of your site. The wine bottle seal in this photo, bearing the name I. DIES, and the date, 1748, not only helped us to learn the age of the site, but we were able to track down the original owner of the bottle!

manufacturer's marking. Those containing markings should be bagged and labeled separately so that they are readily accessible for the purposes of identification after cleaning.

Of all the relics we have been able to find, those that are non-metallic are the most easily cleaned, and while they are often fragile and fragmentary, their pieces remain fairly uncorrupted by the use of modern fertilizers and weed killers used in the fields today. Such is sadly not the case when dealing with metallic relics.

Metallic Relics

There are a lot of theories and ideas dealing with the cleaning of metallic relics and the stabilization of the particular metals. We can get as detailed and complicated about the best ways of doing this, but the typical relic hunter does not have the availability of a laboratory complete with a vast array of exotic chemicals.

Working under the assumption that simple is often better, and that readily available materials will allow the relic hunter the ability to stabilize the metal artifacts he has recovered, I offer these few observations and experiences in the cleaning and stabilization of the most common metals we encounter in the field.

Iron

Iron presents some particular difficulties when recovered in the field. How we go about cleaning this metal depends on the artifact itself. If we are dealing with a cannonball, covered with rust nodules, the cleaning process is simple. Remember, a cannonball was designed to fly through the air and strike a target, after being propelled by an explosive charge. It is almost indestructible, and few things you can dream up are going to harm it. On cannonballs, grapeshot and mortar bomb fragments, the application of the working end of a hammer is usually enough to break off the large clumps of rust that are often attached and any associated flakes on the surface. The ball is then rubbed with coarse steel wool and given several applications of WD-40 and allowed to dry.

Cannonballs are among the most sought after relics and certainly the most easy to clean and preserve.

Belt axes and bayonets are NOT indestructible and greater care must be taken with these types of iron relics. Observe carefully how much deterioration has taken place over the years and note any particular weak areas. The judicious application of a wire wheel will remove most of the surface rust. In areas where more deterioration has taken place, it is to your advantage and the preservation of the intact relic, to use a high speed Dremel tool with a small wire wheel. Remember, we are not out to POLISH the metal as much as to remove flaky surface rust. Once again, as with the cannonball, although using more care, rub the relic with steel wool and again apply repeated coats of WD-40 and allow it to dry.

In the case of very delicate iron objects, the utmost care must be taken, and in some cases, it will be almost impossible to remove all of the rust. Using a magnifying glass and a dental pick, carefully remove all soil and rust nodules. Using a high speed Dremel and a soft wire wheel, very carefully remove as much of the surface flaking as possible, and again, stabilize the iron using WD-40 spray. Using this technique, I have been able to successfully clean and stabilize the metal on several complete Brown Bess gun locks. Never overestimate the strength of the iron relic you are attempting to preserve...always go for the lighter tool and the gentler cleaning method whenever you are in doubt. Never force the cleaning process—and remember that before you apply STRENGTH, apply PATIENCE.

Brass and Copper

A number of the relics recovered in the field will be composed of these two metals. Often they will be found with a deep green and glossy patina. If found with these characteristics, simply clean them using a mild soap solution and leave them alone. They are old...they look old, and the metal has already been stabilized through a natural process. If, however, the metal is covered with a flaky green oxidation that detracts from the relic's appearance, a greater display value can be achieved. Soak the relic in olive oil. The olive oil will begin to dissolve the flaky green coating. This process can take days and the relic should be checked on a regular basis. If it appears that all of the oxidation will not be dissolved by the oil, use a high speed Dremel on those areas where the corrosion is the toughest. The relic will attain a dull brownish-gray color and will achieve a nicer visual effect for your display.

Do not attempt to straighten out bent buckles or other delicate brass or copper relics. Over the years the metal has become brittle and even though the relic looks as though a little pressure will straighten out its lines, it will probably crack. A slightly bent, but intact buckle is far better than several buckle fragments!

47

Cooking pot fragments are commonly found around colonial dwellings and forts. The darker ones have been cleaned of surface rust and sprayed with WD-40, while the rest await cleaning and treatment.

Pewter

Relics composed of pewter are both the most easily corrupted and most highly prized colonial finds made by relic hunters, especially when found in the form of regimentally marked buttons. Fertilizers and other chemicals applied during the farming process, in addition to the constant rotating in the soil, wreaks havoc with this metal and I cannot possibly over-emphasize the great care that is necessary, nor the extreme patience to be employed, when attempting to clean this metal.

In the case of marked buttons, the metal is often cracked, brittle and porous. Even excessive handling of the button can cause edge flaking and the destruction of the loop. Very carefully, and gently, rinse the button under cold water while brushing lightly across the face with a toothbrush to remove any adhering soil. Allow the relic to dry and examine it carefully under a magnifying glass or jeweler's loop. Every step of the way a judgement call must be made. Is it clean enough? Can I possibly get more detail on the face of the button? Be conservative and don't press your luck. A dental pick can be used to remove some additional soil that may clog the details, but it should only be applied with the utmost care. When the cleaning process has been completed to your satisfaction, a thin veneer of Vaseline petroleum jelly can be swabbed onto the surface. Use another cotton swab to remove any excess jelly and display immediately in a glass front, cotton lined display case to prevent any additional handling. The pewter button should not be displayed in any situation where it will move or roll around in the case, as this may lead to additional edge flaking.

Pewter regimental buttons are important sources of information about troops occupying certain locations. They are very delicate and should be handled with great care during the cleaning process.

When in the field, it is always wise to carry some 35mm film cases with cotton balls inside them. If a pewter button is recovered, it should be immediately placed between two cotton balls and secured within the film case. Under no circumstances is a delicate relic such as this to be placed in the collecting bag with other heavy relics as its destruction will become inevitable.

Lead

One of the most common and easily cleaned metal relics are composed of lead. To clean musketballs or other lead objects, a little lukewarm water and mild soap will quickly do the trick. The desired effect is a nice white patina of thin oxidation. No scrubbing is necessary, although you might want to roll them around while they are soaking in the bottom of a tray.

Lead objects are very common recoveries and easily cleaned in lukewarm water. Chewed musketballs and lead pencils are routinely found at sites once occupied by early forts.

As with your recovered non-metallic relics, metal relics should be labeled according to where they were found and the date and period to which they relate. Clear fishing lure cases come in many sizes, with numerous compartments and are an ideal way of keeping your relics in order according to their sites of recovery.

In Summary

The cleaning and stabilization of your relics is an essential part of being a relic hunter. I have seen situations where important relics have simply been thrown into a cardboard box with little regard to cleaning or preventing their further deterioration. On the other hand, I have seen overly enthusiastic cleaning done where a sandblaster or tumbler was employed with the results of nearly destroying relics of importance. Going to either of these extremes denotes a lack of care and understanding of what these individual relics represent and the story they can tell. It is of great importance that we use extreme and judicious care while preserving these historical reminders of the past.

Chapter 5

Relic Identification

The research that enabled us to find the site is over, as is our relic hunt. We have recovered a number of interesting relics and have gone through the various processes to clean them. We have labeled them as to the location of discovery. In some cases it is easy to tell what these relics are, but in other cases, those fragmentary finds offer us another challenge—identification.

Identifying your finds can be a long and grueling task, but usually results in a growing knowledge of your site and no small amount of fun. A box of unknown relics is just so much scrap metal until its story is revealed through identification.

Something as seemingly insignificant as a nail, when properly identified, can help to narrow down the era of a site you have discovered, while a single button may contain a wealth of information as to the troops who garrisoned an outpost. The act of recovery is only a small portion of what motivates the relic hunter or lures him to the wooded slopes or a stubbled cornfield...it is the thirst for knowledge about our common past that is quenched through our efforts of recovery, preservation, and identification. Whether your interest compels you to search sites from the French and Indian War, the American Revolution or the Civil War, the drive and passions are the same.

When it comes to identification, it is back to "hitting the books." Your research library will be of little help during this portion of the hunt. No single book will contain all of the information you seek, and you'll find your library of identification books growing quickly as more specific information is desired.

I guess the first question any relic hunter would ask would be,

"Where do we acquire these books that will help us with the process of identification?" Very few town libraries or local book stores carry the books necessary for the task ahead of us, but the easiest way to get a good beginner's identification library started would be by purchasing the Dixie Gun Works catalog. The price of this telephone book sized catalog is four dollars and, pound for pound, it is a great source of information, offering a wide selection of books you might need to add to your identification library. The address is DIXIE GUN WORKS, INC., GUN POWDER LANE, UNION CITY, TENNESSEE 32861, or simply call 1-800-238-6785 to order your copy.

Between the covers of the catalog you will find a book section complete with descriptions of each selection. Identification books contained in the catalog run from the general to the very specific and range from the very earliest times to the modern day. Books on arms, equipment, uniforms, edged weapons, military tactics, campaigns and personalities abound.

For the relic hunter whose primary interest is in the colonial era, the best work, and one I've used on thousands of occasions, is the COLLECTOR'S ILLUSTRATED ENCYCLOPEDIA OF THE AMERICAN REVOLUTION by George C. Neumann and Frank J. Kravic. This masterful work contains more than 2,300 illustrations of Revolutionary War era relics, with a majority of them having been excavated. I consider this book to be the "keystone" for relic identification of this period.

For American buttons of all periods, including buttons of the South during the Civil War period, the primary source of identification is the RECORD OF AMERICAN UNIFORM AND HISTORICAL BUTTONS by Alphaeus H. Albert, while the classic work on British buttons for the Revolutionary War period would have to be HISTORY WRITTEN WITH PICK AND SHOVEL by Calver and Bolton, originally published by the New York Historical Society and reprinted in 1970. Remember that pipe fragment we found on the site of the stockaded fort...the one with the cartouche bearing the initials R-TIP-PET? Using the book by Calver and Bolton, we were easily able to identify it as dating from the mid 1700s and having been manufactured in Bristol, England!

The more you are involved in relic hunting, the larger your ID library will become. Knowing what you have found, and how it was used, is the keystone of information for the relic hunter.

Many of the relics we recover are found in only a partial state, and as such, are often more difficult to identify. Looking at each fragment with an analytical eye, we attempt to establish the purpose of its design. The thickness and type of metal will often give us some indication as to whether the object was decorative or functional. Some relics may take years and a bit of luck to identify.

There have been a number of occasions when I have been out hunting with fellow relic hunters and we've stumbled upon a site that produced some unusual finds that defied a quick, field identification, and knowing that hours would be spent solving the ID problem was a way of actually extending the thrill of the hunt. There have also been those times which have caused me a certain amount of sadness, when I've witnessed important historic finds thrown into a "junk box" because the relic hunter didn't take the time to identify and label his finds. As relic hunters we have an obligation to record the story our recoveries tell and proper identification is a key to unraveling the mysteries of our country's past.

These brass keg spigots, recovered on the site of a colonial tavern, were clearly identified as period pieces. (Courtesy of George C. Neumann)

In the following section of this chapter I have listed various books that can help the relic hunter to identify some of his finds. I have listed them according to the periods of time in which most relic hunters are interested. A few of the books will overlap certain periods of interest and when this occurs, I have noted it in parentheses following the listing. Some of these books will be difficult to find, and some may be out of print. At times tracking down a needed text on identification is similar to tracking down a new site to search...it's just another of the challenges facing the relic hunter!

COLONIAL AND REVOLUTIONARY WAR PERIOD

Albert, Alphaeus H., RECORD OF AMERICAN UNI-FORM AND HISTORICAL BUTTONS-Bicentennial Edition, Boyertown Publishing Co., Boyertown, Pennsylvania, 1976. (Military buttons of all periods)

Calver, W. L. and Bolton, R. P., HISTORY WRITTEN WITH PICK AND SHOVEL, New York Historical Society, New York, 3rd printing, 1970. (Some War of 1812 period relics included.)

Hamilton, T. M., COLONIAL FRONTIER GUNS, Pioneer Press, Union City, Tennessee, 1987.

Hamilton, T. M., FIREARMS OF THE FRONTIER: GUNS AT FORT MICHILIMACKINAC 1715-1781, Reports in Mackinac History and Archaeology, Number 5, Mackinac Island State Park Commission, Williamston, Michigan, 1976.

Hanson, Lee and Hsu, Dick Ping, CASEMATES AND CANNONBALLS: ARCHAEOLOGICAL INVESTIGATIONS AT FORT STANWIX, ROME, NEW YORK, Publications in Archeology 14, U. S. Department of the Interior, National Park Service, Washington, D. C., 1975.

Hume, Ivor Noel, A GUIDE TO ARTIFACTS OF COLONIAL AMERICA, Vintage Books edition, 1991.

Moore, Warren, WEAPONS OF THE AMERICAN REVOLUTION AND ACCOUTREMENTS, Promontory Press, New York, 1967.

Neumann, George C., SWORDS AND BLADES OF THE AMERICAN REVOLUTION, 3rd edition, Rebel Publishing Co., Inc., Texarkana, TX, 1991.

Neumann, George C., and Kravic, Frank J., COLLECTOR'S ILLUSTRATED ENCYCLOPEDIA OF THE AMERICAN REVOLUTION, Rebel Publishing Co., Inc., Texarkana, TX, 1989.

Peterson, Harold L., THE BOOK OF THE CONTINEN-TAL SOLDIER, Stackpole Company, Harrisburg, Pennsylvania, 1968.

Sprouse, Deborah A., A GUIDE TO EXCAVATED CO-LONIAL AND REVOLUTIONARY WAR ARTIFACTS, Heritage Trails, Turbotville, Pennsylvania, 1988

Sullivan, Catherine, LEGACY OF THE MACHAULT: A COLLECTION OF 18TH CENTURY ARTIFACTS, available through: Canadian Government Publishing Centre, Supply and Services Canada, Hull. Quebec, Canada, K1A 0S9

WAR OF 1812

Campbell, Duncan J. and Howell, Edgar M., AMERICAN MILITARY INSIGNIA 1800-1851, Confederate States Press, Baton Rouge, LA. Smithsonian Institution, Bulletin 235, Washington, D. C., 1963.

Chartrand, Rene, UNIFORMS AND EQUIPMENT OF THE U. S. FORCES IN THE WAR OF 1812, Old Fort Niagara Association, Inc., Youngstown, New York, 1992.

Katcher, Philip, ARMIES OF THE AMERICAN WARS 1753-1815, Hastings House Publishers, New York, 1975. (French and Indian War, American Revolution, War of 1812)

THE CIVIL WAR

Kerksis, Sydney C., PLATES AND BUCKLES OF THE AMERICAN MILITARY 1795-1874, Stone Mountain Press, Stone Mountain, Georgia, 3rd edition, 1987. (Includes War of 1812)

Lord, Francis A., CIVIL WAR COLLECTOR'S ENCYCLOPEDIA, volumes I-V, Lord Americana and Research, Inc., W. Columbia, South Carolina, 1963-1989.

McKee, W. Reid, and Mason, M. E. Jr., CIVIL WAR PROJECTILES II: SMALL ARMS AND FIELD ARTILLERY, Moss Publications, Orange, Virginia, 1980.

NORTH SOUTH TRADERS CIVIL WAR COLLECTORS' PRICE GUIDE, 6th Edition, North South Traders Civil War, Orange, Virginia, 1993

Phillips, Stanley S., EXCAVATED ARTIFACTS FROM BATTLEFIELDS AND CAMPSITES OF THE CIVIL WAR 1861-1865, Walsworth Publishing Co., Marceline, Missouri, 5th printing, 1986.

Sylvia, Stephen W. and O'Donnell, Michael J., ILLUS-
TRATED HISTORY OF CIVIL WAR RELICS, Moss Publications, Orange, Virginia, 3rd publication, 1988.

Remember, IDENTIFICATION should not be considered
a time consuming task, but a way of getting more information
about your site, while at the same time learning substantially more
about the period of time in which you are interested. Using the
texts I have mentioned in this chapter, you should encounter very
little difficulty in identifying your relic recoveries. Identification
is only a small part of the "book work" needed in relic hunting and
as opposed to the history "homework" you once struggled
through—this is FUN!

Displaying Your Finds

Once your relics have been cleaned and identified, a way of
displaying them should be considered. Obviously, your own tastes
will play a major role in how this is accomplished, as well as space
constraints and the size of your collection. I have seen some
beautiful displays, complete with labeled tags and artwork, representative of the search period, accompanying the relics in glass
and wood cases. A display of this type is highly effective for small
relics.

For larger artifacts, the relic hunter might consider a large
frame of weathered barn siding, which can be anchored on a wall.
This will enable you to save a good deal of space and still effec-
tively display your relic recoveries to their best advantage. If a
large number of relics have been recovered from one particular
site, they should be grouped together. Engraved brass tags, stating
the history of the site, can be used to enhance the total effect of
your display.

Open shelf displays are effective, as well, but there are some
things to consider before taking that course of action. One of

Organizing and displaying your recovered relics allows others to appreciate their historic significance. Finds made on the same site should be kept together and labeled accordingly.

these considerations is maintenance...continually dusting relics can be a laborious and time consuming chore. Also, if there are children in the house, this can be the worst possible type of display to employ...not only because of the danger involved in a child's handling certain relics, but due to loss. A relic hunting buddy of mine frequently has his young grandaughter over to his house. On one occasion, he found her spitting something out on the carpet— what she thought were candies in a bowl, were actually musketballs displayed in half a mortar bomb which was sitting on his shelf. The bayonet dating from the French and Indian War, and bent to form a pot hanger for campfire cooking...well, it's been eight years now and he STILL hasn't found it! A word to the wise should be sufficient.

Chapter 6

Documenting the Site

Record keeping is another facet of relic hunting that should not be ignored. Even something as simple as keeping a journal in a composition book and recording each particular hunt will be helpful when you desire to return to search the site in later years. This can be especially helpful for relic hunts conducted on farmlands. The conditions of the field should be carefully noted. When was the field plowed? When was the field harvested? What types of crops are currently planted?

Answers to these questions will help you to plan your arrival at the site to coincide with the plowing or harvesting the following year. There are few things more frustrating to a relic hunter than arriving at a site just BEFORE the fields have been harvested and not being able to work the site for fear of doing damage to any standing crops. While the farmer will be very congenial about allowing you to work his land when it is free of growing crops, it can be quite a different story when he senses damage being done to his livelihood. If the farmer gives his approval to work his fields when they are planted, special note of this should be entered into your journal.

The types of finds that are made during a particular hunt should be noted, as well as any areas of concentrated relics. In doing these types of entries, be sure to note any landmarks that will allow you to place yourself in the exact spot during the following season. When a field has been re-plowed and a different crop has been planted, the old field, which was so familiar to you, will take on a whole new aspect in later years. Be aware of this, and make notes that will insure your continued success on the site.

Over a decade ago, while researching the site of a fort we

wanted to relic hunt, we ran across the fact that the fort had been attacked by a group of French soldiers and their Indian allies. In written accounts of the attack, we could plainly see that it had originated in the northwest section of the surrounding fields. The accounts related how the fort "responded with grape and round shot" from its eighteen pound cannons.

Following our search of the fort site, we headed into the fields to see if we could locate any cannonballs or grape shot. Our initial attempts met with failure, but just before winter we stumbled on a small area that was riddled with grape shot. By the end of that hunt we were able to recover almost two hundred pieces of shot. I knew that more would probably be turned up the following year and I wanted to be sure I would once again be able to find that exact point in those broad fields. There were no readily available landmarks and each rolling hill in the field looked like the next.

Noting where the grape shot had been most concentrated, I began pacing off the distance from the center of the grape shot concentration to the edge of the river. Traveling in a straight line, due east, I walked ninety-five paces before I came to a large tree on the bank of the river. Taking some large stones that had been thrown on the edge of the field, I stacked them at the base of the tree to mark it. There were many trees along the banks of the river and I didn't want to take any chances about remembering which was the right one. Looking back across the field, I saw a house directly across from me about a quarter of a mile in the distance. All of these observations and measurements were re-corded in my journal of the hunt, along with a diagram of the site.

As things would have it, I did not return to the site for almost ten years. The night before our return hunt, I pulled out my old journal a re-read my notes on the site of the fort. During that reading, I also noted the area where the grape shot had been found. I hoped I would be able to find it once again.

While my partner searched the area that would have been the interior of the fort, I hunted along the trees on the banks of the river for my marker. Finding it, I paced off ninety-five strides, due west, in the direction of the house I had earlier noted. I turned on my detector and within five minutes, I was able to find the first of many newly recovered rounds of grape shot. As you can see, journal entries are an important record that will be able to aid you in your future searches on a site. You may not be able to make it back to the site the following season and MEMORY is not always a trustworthy tool for the relic hunter.

Depending on how important you perceive your site to be, your note taking and documentation should be detailed accordingly. This is especially true when you are searching a structure...the site of an old fort, the cellar hole remains of a colonial home, or a winter encampment containing the remains of huts.

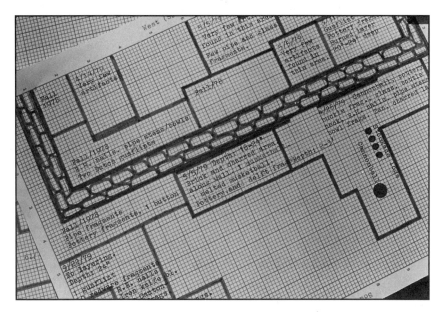

The charting of a blockhouse site dating from the colonial wars, enabled us to keep an accurate record of recoveries. Along with a written account of each hunt on the site, a clear picture of historic events began to emerge.

Remember those western blockhouses at the site of the fort we hunted in an earlier chapter? Well, our research revealed that the foundation of each blockhouse was twenty-four feet square. To establish exactly where the foundation remains were, in relation to the recovered artifacts, we decided to use a seven foot probe. While the surface of the field in that area was strewn with foundation stones, there was no pattern to them...however...below the plow-line, the remains of the foundation were still intact. By marking each solid hit with the probe, the pattern revealed itself and an accurate chart could be made of that particular feature of the fort. By knowing the approximate size of the fort, and by working from the exact location of the foundation we had measured, it was easily possible for us to draw an accurate representation of the entire fort site.

When attempting to document the site of a temporary encampment a good diagram or map of the area under search is important. Be sure to note permanent features such as rock ledges, boulders and nearby streams. Once again, note areas where the artifacts were recovered in relation to each one of these permanent features, and in relation to each other. The finding of small pieces of melted lead found in relation to several unclipped balls would suggest the area of the encampment where the casting of musketballs took place. All of these small bits of information are important to your growing understanding of the site.

While recently searching the area of a temporary encampment, I happened upon a section of ground that contained almost a dozen fired musketballs. That tiny section could have been covered by your typical garbage can lid. What did that recovery suggest? It seemed pretty unmistakable that colonial troops had been enjoying a little target practice. Knowing where the target had been set up, and the approximate range of a musket, I was able to find the area of the firing line and recover some dropped balls along with a few colonial era pewter buttons. All of these features and finds were noted on my chart of the site as well as in my

These French and Indian war era axes were recovered at the site of a temporary encampment.

written account of the relic hunt.

Don't believe for a second that you will not have any need for records and that you will never return to a site because it has been hunted out. In the situation of working plowed fields, the "crop" of relics in the soil is constantly on the move between the plow-line and the surface, and even the depth of the plow-line, from season to season, can change, depending on the weather and the different types of crops that are being planted. I know of several sites that have been worked by literally an army of relic hunters and each year new and interesting finds are being made. The frequency of the finds may be less and the targets may be smaller, but nonetheless, it remains a site to be searched.

In the case of relic bearing grounds that have not seen the influence of the plow, new detector advances in technology are producing recovery depths that we only dreamed about a decade ago. Using the notes and charts I made ten years ago, and armed with the technological advances in modern detectors, I am revisiting and re-hunting many of the sites I had once thought to have been "played out"...and better relic recoveries are being made.

Taking the time to make notes and maps on a site is important. It insures that our discoveries, both in terms of relics and information, are not lost, as well as being an important and primary reference tool for future hunts on the site. TAKE NOTES...MAKE MAPS...AND YOUR KNOWLEDGE OF THE SITE AND PERIOD OF TIME WILL DOUBLE WITH THE RECOVERY OF ADDITIONAL RELICS.

Chapter 7

Ground Conditions & Relic Hunting Techniques

"Working the Land"

More than in any other form of detecting, relic hunting will provide you with a number of challenges when it comes to ground conditions. With relic hunting, smooth, level and grassy hunting sites will be the exception rather than the rule. You can anticipate the unexpected. Developing and using a variety of detecting techniques will help to insure your success in the field.

As mentioned in an earlier chapter, dressing for these different and often difficult situations you will find yourself in is of optimum importance. You can expect to be entangled by vines, and scratched by thorns...bitten by mosquitoes and be the subject of interest to the local tick population. Knowing beforehand and being prepared for these minor inconveniences of the field is essential.

Dense Brush

Heavy brush can probably be expected on a majority of the sites you will be searching, and working in it can present some particular challenges. Relic hunting in brushy areas requires the use of all your limbs and manual dexterity seldom witnessed outside a circus arena.

Since brushy ground will make it difficult, if not impossible, to swing your coil across the surface, the tangles of brush must be flattened out with your boots. Once the brush is securely underfoot, it is possible to sweep over them in your search for a target.

It is an arduously slow process...left boot—FLATTEN...right boot—FLATTEN...SWEEP...SWEEP...SWEEP. Searching slowly, and keeping your lateral sweeping of the coil to a minimum width, will allow you to progress through the tangle. It is also advisable to shorten the length of the detector pole while searching under such conditions. Don't expect to speed through this type of ground coverage. Be patient.

Heavy Weeds

If you are searching an area of heavy weeds, you might consider the same technique you used on brush, however, a good golf club-like weed wacker will often do the trick. While recently working a homesite dating from the late 1700s, I used one of these weed wackers to help in the recovery of several early large cents and other relics associated with the era of the home. Where the weeds were less dense, I would swing the weed wacker with my left hand and then sweep my detector across the newly cut area with my right. In areas where the weeds were of a more dense nature, I would put the detector down for a couple of minutes while I cleared the area to be searched and then went over it with the detector.

In certain situations, especially if we are encountering very tall and thick grass, it would probably be better to leave that area of the search or postpone the hunt until the very early spring, before the grass has an opportunity to reach any great height.

Slopes - Rocky and Otherwise

Relic hunting slopes for any extended period of time can present particular challenges to your physical endurance. Your technique should vary according to what is most comfortable to you. When you are working a slope from its base to summit, the detector pole should be shortened, and while you will not be sweeping the coil over as much ground, you will find the short-

The remains of a cellar hole, dating from 1796, could barely be seen through the dense tangle of weeds. Such conditions present a challenge to any relic hunter.

ened detector easier to use. This is especially true when you have to dig a target on a slope. It is a nerve-wracking experience to feel your headset being pulled from your head as you watch a nine hundred dollar detector sliding and rolling down the face of a hill. When you are kneeling to dig your target, you'll also find the shortened detector easier to handle when you are pinpointing.

On short slopes, where each leg of the pattern will be less than two hundred feet, I like to search from the base to the summit and then walk down to the base and begin the next leg of the search pattern to the summit once again. I find that I have greater control and am less likely to take a spill when working in this fashion. When searching slopes, balance is a key and you'll find your ankles working double-time to keep you even and upright. When digging targets, always remember to face toward the summit of the slope. The steeper the grade of the slope, the more impossible it will become to dig a target when facing toward the base of the hill.

When relic hunting for a "hot spot" on the face of hills, my partner and I will generally spread ourselves a distance apart and run our search patterns in a parallel fashion as we traverse the slope. I generally keep the pole assembly fully extended in a search of this nature, and in employing a search style or strategy of this type, we will be able to cover a far greater amount of land as we attempt to find a relic laden area.

Rocky slopes present some difficulty in that many of your targets will be covered by slabs of rocks that have slid down the face of the slope over the years. If you go over a rock and your detector registers a target signal don't anticipate that you have found a "hot rock", as your target probably can be found in the depths of the soil below the rock.

Several years ago, my partner detected what he thought to be a hot rock. Not having encountered any of these on the slopes that day, I asked him to show me where it was. Passing the coil of my detector over the slab resulted in an ear wrenching signal.

From six inches below the flat stone we removed half of an eight inch mortar bomb dating from the French and Indian War!

An important warning should also be mentioned. When working rocky slopes, or any rocky area, for that matter, NEVER PUT YOUR HANDS ANYWHERE THAT YOU CAN'T SEE. During that same hunt and following the recovery of the mortar bomb, my partner was reaching between two large stones to retrieve a target. Not being able to recover it in that fashion, he decided to remove one of the large, flat slabs of stone...beneath the stone, and coiling about so very playfully, was a nest of baby timber rattlers. A word to the wise should be sufficient.

From The Land To The Water's Edge

Many of the sites you will be searching will be in close proximity to a water source. The water may be in the form of a pond, river, or stream. The slope of land between the area where you have found earlier relics and the edge of the water will be one of the most difficult and most productive areas to search. The water source was used by troops for cooking, drinking, bathing and washing purposes, and as such, has become the repository of eating utensils, buttons, musketballs, canteens and other assorted camp equipment. In many cases, these slopes were also a convenient way of getting rid of worn and broken equipment. Many camp dumps are found along such slopes, and you should check these areas carefully.

It would probably also be advisable to hip-mount your detector, throw on a pair of chest or hip waders and extend your hunt INTO the water for a few yards, as currents and waves may have leached some of the relics from the slope into the water just off the shoreline. Recoveries made under these conditions are time-consuming, but once you have found an area that is producing relics from your period of interest, you want to work all of the angles.

The "hardware of history" can be found in the least likely places. The two smaller axe blades were recovered at the water's edge. Both were recovered during the summer months when the water level was lower. During the fall and spring they would have been submerged.

During a recent hunt at a river side colonial fort dating from 1755, my partner was able to recover a British "broad arrow" stamped camp axe and a small cannonball from a swivel gun, along with a large assortment of early relics dating from the period of the fort. The bank was weed clogged and covered with thorny brush, but the recoveries he was able to make were certainly worth his efforts.

The Forest and Woodlands

When searching forests and woodlands it is often difficult to establish a precise pattern for your search as you work your way between the trees. Normally, you won't find too much ground cover or brush to inhibit your search, so the ability to swing your coil will usually be done with little difficulty. When you find an area that begins to bear relics, establish limits to your hunt and work as tight a pattern as possible.

Hidden deep in the woods, we found and searched the remains of a colonial quarry.

One of the greatest difficulties you will encounter in this setting is the retrieving of targeted relics through a matrix and webbing of roots. The roots you will encounter in brushy areas will appear as nothing in comparison to the thick roots of the forest. Finding the relic will often not be as difficult as recovering it, and the act of recovery, especially on large and very deep targets, can be played out over an extended period of time.

I recall one particular incident where I had targeted a very large relic. From previous recoveries I sensed it was a cannonball. Working through the webbing of roots, first with my digger and then my entrenching tool, I was finally able to approach the target through the soil. Growing over and around the upper surface of the cannonball were two roots, each as thick as my forearm.

Peering into the hole I was just able to make out the roots and the round upper curve of the ball sixteen inches below. I knew it would be impossible to retrieve a relic of that size from beneath those roots using the original hole. Knowing I would never leave a relic of that type unrecovered, I sat back and thought about how to best accomplish the task ahead of me. I decided to angle a second hole, from the other side of the large roots, in an attempt to work my way below the ball and have it drop down into the newly dug tunnel beneath it. After an hour of digging the task was completed and I was able to wrestle the eighteen pound cannonball to the surface. It had taken time, but a successful recovery was made. It was the best find I made that day, and certainly well worth my strenuous efforts!

Recovered from deep within the forest floor, this cannonball made it to the light of day after almost two and a half centuries!

Relic Hunting "Hammered" Sites

It is very easy to tell when you are searching a site that has been relic hunted in the past. Depending on how heavily it was hunted, the nature of your finds will vary. If a site has really been "hammered", the resulting recovered relics will be small and deep. This is where your large coil and modern technology will pay dividends. Overlapping both your sweep and your search pattern will help you to recover any relics that have been left in the ground.

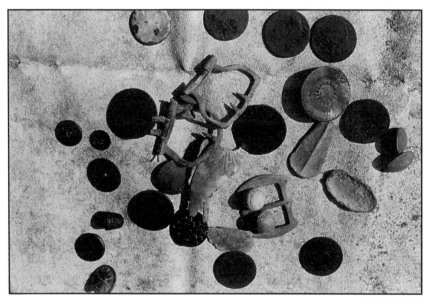

"Hammered" site recoveries are usually small and deep. These recovered relics were found on a heavily worked common dating from the late 1700s.

In some cases, it may be to your benefit to relic hunt with a small coil in heavily worked areas, as previous metal detector operators, using large coils, may have rejected a good target that was lying in the ground in close association with small ferrous objects such as nails. The key element when working "hammered" sites is to experiment and play hunches. Don't expect to find a large number of relics in an area of the site that is most easily hunted...everybody has been there before you. Take some chances and try working those areas where it appears to be the most difficult to hunt. Thick brush, rocky slopes, and embankments, that can only be searched with the greatest of patience, will produce relics that other hunters have missed. "Moving the furniture," is a term I often use when it comes to clearing broken limbs and rotten tree trunks from an area I want to search. These areas provide a limited, but often productive avenue for recovering relics missed by searchers who have detected the site before you. Take the time to move some of the fallen debris that obstructs a thorough search of the site.

No matter what ground conditions you encounter on your relic site, it is possible to complete the day with a successful hunt by being patient and trying a few new techniques. Remember to keep your thinking out of the rut previous relic hunters might have employed when they searched the site...experiment, improvise, and play your hunches!

Chapter 8

Military Relic Sites

"What To Look For and How To Find Them"

There are quite a number of different types of military sites for which relic hunters search. Many of these sites will be found very near to the area in which you live, and a little research, accompanied by a little leg work—some intuition with a dash of deductive reasoning and logic...will lead you on to a successful relic hunt.

When looking for particular types of relic sites there are certain characteristics and qualities that must be noted in the features of the earth. Many vestiges of the past linger on, written in the surface of the soil and being able to read the often subtle story, diminished in its nature by the passage of time, is one of the other challenges facing the relic hunter.

Being able to "get inside the head" of someone who lived centuries ago, being able to think like a general and then like a private, will help you to understand the terrain you are about to search. History does provide us with some written clues, but a lot has to be left up to the imagination and creativity of the individual relic hunter.

Temporary Encampments

Major Robert Rogers, leader of the ranger corp that bore his name during the French and Indian War, gives us some very particular information on the establishing of a temporary camp. In his journal Rogers cites several criteria for placing a camp. His advice is based on a battlefield logic that remains true to this day, and knowing areas through which troops moved, when viewed in the light of his reasoning, will help us to find likely places where temporary camps were positioned. In his own words, Rogers advises to "March until quite dark before encamping; which do, on a piece of ground which will afford the sentinels an opportunity of seeing and hearing the enemy at a considerable distance." In other passages in his journal, Rogers often refers to encamping near sources of water, usually a stream or brook.

Basically, by following Rogers' thinking, we would be looking for any eminence that allowed for a good panoramic view of the surrounding terrain which was located near a stream. Knowing his line of march, and by using his advice, could put the relic hunter on the site of one of his encampments.

Rogers also mentions, in several passages, encamping on high ridges overlooking forts and permanent forward posts set up by the French. Establishing where the forts or posts were located, and checking a topographic map of the area, will make likely encampments easy to find...at least on paper. A good deal of strenuous leg work and the checking of several sites may be necessary before finding an encampment.

A temporary evening encampment was generally a small affair and not likely to have seen much continued use. Rangers and scouts did not like to return to the same site with any sort of frequency due to the fact that it would be too easy for enemy troops to set up an ambush once the site had been discovered. The disadvantage to the relic hunter in searching these types of sites is in the form of a limited number of relics. The advantages, however, are that there were many of these types of sites, and the relics recovered, since the grounds will not have ever been plowed, will generally be found in a very good state of preservation.

When encamping behind their own lines, large masses of troops would usually travel by roads cut through the forest, and encampments can be found near the fords of streams and creeks where the roads crossed. In many cases, when a very good encampment site was found, it was repeatedly used, and in some cases, became a permanent encampment or post, which witnessed the coming and going of troops on almost a daily basis.

Troops traveling by water would usually encamp on points of land that jutted into a river or lake. This was done for one simple reason, defense. Being in a position that was surrounded by water on three sides made a successful defense of the position more likely and offered a good view of enemy movements across the surface of the body of water. When looking for temporary encampments, ALL points of land should be thoroughly checked.

Found in the deep woods on the sites of temporary encampments and small military installations, these buckles, thimbles, and lead pencil, offer the relic hunter a unique glimpse into the past.

When searching a likely encampment site, I like to use my hottest, deepest seeking detector with a large coil. As it is unlikely that I will be bothered by small ferrous targets, such as nails, I run with minimum discrimination, while the sensitivity approaches maximum levels. Initial searches are done with a loose pattern until a relic recovery has been made, then a tight search pattern is run over the "hot spot" and surrounding ground.

The reasoning used in establishing campsites changed little over the centuries and the same logic applies whether you are searching for those of the French and Indian War as well as the Civil War.

Permanent Encampments And Forward Outposts

Permanent encampments often took on the appearances of a "mini-fort" and were usually set up along wilderness roadways between larger installations such as forts. As with temporary encampments, a source of water was an essential and many of these more permanent encampments can be found adjacent to creeks and rivers.

Often, while conducting a visual search of the suspected grounds, telltale signs will still remain on the surface. In some instances, lengthy depressions forming right angles will denote a stockaded wall that has deteriorated. As the log walls rotted, the surrounding earth caved in, forming a noticeable depression. In other cases, earthen walls were thrown up around the site, and these will still be easily noted in the form of small rises running for some length around the site.

Outside the remains of the walls you may find another line of depressions. Many times these shallow depressions represent a first line of defense in the form of rifle pits or trenches. By the same token, larger depressions found within the walls could be representative of hut sites used by the troops stationed at the post. The areas around each should be thoroughly searched.

Forward outposts were used as "listening" or observation posts to a larger installation. They were generally manned by small garrisons on a rotating basis and guarded the approaches to a fort.

These approaches may have been along a roadway, bridge head, or a waterway. Maps and diagrams of the larger installation will often include these outposts and approaches and they should be carefully noted when revealed through your research.

If few clues to the site exist on the surface of the land, begin your metal detecting search in much the same fashion employed with a hunt on a temporary encampment...minimal discrimination and maximum sensitivity. The exact site of the outpost will become apparent with the chatter of small ferrous targets, as numerous nails will often litter the site. Once the exact location of the outpost has been established, you may increase your discrimination to avoid a majority of the nails. However, remember that pewter will be one of the next metals you will lose if you increase your discrimination setting too high.

Forts

Forts are among the most well documented sites in history. They are also likely to have been reconstructed by private or governmental agencies depending on their historic value. In many cases, the more prominent the installation, the more likely it is to be protected by federal and state historic preservation laws.

However, many forts, while serving to protect small communities and being of paramount significance in the past, remain today as little more than a footnote in history. Many of the remains of these forts linger beneath the plowed surfaces of farmers' fields. They are on private lands and once permission for the search has been granted, are perfectly legal to search.

A visual survey of the suspected site will reveal several relic indicators. These will usually be in the form of pipe fragments, broken pottery and glass, brick fragments and foundation stones. Once you turn on your detector the overwhelming chatter, when relic hunting with your discrimination levels at a minimum, will become an overpowering nuisance, and adjustments to your discrimination and sensitivity levels will be warranted...unless you enjoy digging fifty small ferrous targets for every ten feet of the hunt.

Early fort sites often provide an interesting assembly of recovered relics. Rifle barrel bands, ice creepers, grapeshot, pewter spoons, ramrod tips and pipes are often common finds.

Look for foundation stones representing large features on the site and run your search patterns accordingly. Be sure to check areas where old roadways may once have existed, and if located on a river or lake, any sections of the shoreline that may have been used as a docking area for boats bringing supplies to the installation.

Many forts had areas allotted for the growing of vegetables by the individual soldiers to supplement their government rations. These garden areas should be thoroughly searched as well.

Attempt to visualize how the fort once appeared based on the information you are "reading" on the surface of the ground, and look for likely places where soldiers may have thrown discarded and broken equipment...the closest embankment is a good place to begin your search for a relic riddled dump area.

Being able to pull a bucket of nails from a fort site, is no great feat, however, the style of nail, in this case "rose heads", are good indicators to the age of the site.

Battles And Skirmishes

Once again, in the case of major battles, both state and federal agencies may have set up historic parks. These areas will be OFF LIMITS to the relic hunter. In many cases, these historic parks will range over numerous acres of land. It is perfectly legal, when permission has been granted by a private landowner whose property may be near or adjacent to a historic park, to search his land for relics associated with that particular battle.

Knowing WHERE you are and the boundaries of such a park is of monumental importance...it will keep you out of the judicial system, allow you to retain ownership of your equipment, your car or truck will still be parked in YOUR garage rather than in a federal impound yard, you'll save money by not having to face payment of large fines and you'll sleep far better by not having to worry about who your bunkmate is going to be in a federal prison. NEVER CROSS FEDERAL OR STATE PARK LINES WITH A DETECTOR OR DIGGING TOOL.

With that warning established, you'll be free to search lands where other battles and skirmishes have taken place in the past. In the case of a running battle, where the lines of battle shifted from one area to another, pinning down a particular "hot spot" can only be done with a lot of leg work and swinging. Running loose patterns across a suspected area can result in the recovery of fired projectiles. Once these begin to appear, tighten up your search patterns. Be sure to check areas of depressions where troops may have sought cover. Check the banks of streams where they may have sought refreshment. Check ridges where they may have sought the advantages of height. THINK like a soldier caught in the line of fire.

When researching a battle, be sure to note areas where troops encamped before the battle was fought and places where they retreated to following the bloody contest. The lines of retreat should also be noted as the more hasty the retreat, the more likely it will be to find discarded equipment.

In searching the sites of battles and small, poorly documented skirmishes, a TEAM approach to relic hunting may be desired. With the individual members of the relic hunting team spread apart, the chances of finding a "hot spot" in a broad field or forest is more likely. This team approach is an effective search method, allowing for communication of finds during the hunt, and resulting in less time being wasted while covering unproductive areas. Be sure when asking permission to relic hunt on private property that the landowner is aware of the number of people you expect to have in the field. Receiving permission for ONE does not mean that the property owner will enjoy the fact that you've brought three other relic hunters along with you.

Relic hunting for military artifacts is probably the most exciting and intriguing aspect of using a metal detector. The droning history lectures we were often forced to endure in high school will be all but forgotten in light of holding a piece of history in your hands. Being able to "touch" history is an adventure never found within the covers of those old American History textbooks!

Other Sites - Non-Military

While relic hunting military sites is probably the most exciting type of searching you will do, the domestic side of your period of interest is not without its share of adventure as well.

Searching the grounds around old cellar holes can usually provide the relic hunter with some interesting finds.

Old cellar holes, located in the deep woods, are a primary attraction to relic hunters when the fields are under growing crops and impossible to search. The fact that the original dwelling may have existed on the site for well over a century provides us with a cross section of life that can extend over a long period of time. An opportunity to search an old cellar hole should never be turned down, and the research you do on your local area should be sure to include areas where houses once stood.

Many counties and towns still have old maps dating from the earliest settlements of the area. In many cases, the sites of old homes are drawn in along the roads. Comparing the old maps with new maps of your community can provide the relic hunter with important clues as to where to search.

When searching cellar holes avoid the obvious. Hopping into a cellar hole and searching the floor area will usually result in an amazing number of small iron targets. If the structure rotted away or was reduced by fire, a good portion of the collapsing structure plummeted into the depths of the cellar. However, it is always advisable to check the stone walls of a cellar hole for hidden caches that may have been left behind once the structure was abandoned. Chimney areas and especially large hearth stones are good places to carefully check with your detector.

The closer you work to the outside of the foundation, the more trashy targets you will generally receive. You may want to adjust your discrimination and sensitivity when working close. Be sure to range out and run patterns on all sections that once represented the house site. Remember, as well, that it was usual to have several out-buildings associated with early homes...privies, sheds, barns, chicken coops. In walking to and from these structures, buttons and coins were often lost. Look for slopes that may have provided a dumping area for discarded and broken household items and fixtures. Large areas of intense signals may indicate such a dump, and you may choose to sift through the area rather than attempt to pinpoint and recover individual targets. The

One of the cellar holes at our quarry site had shelves built into the foundation.

recovery of non-metallic artifacts in the form of pottery, glassware and pipe fragments may help you to identify the age of your site.

Individual home sites should be worked very carefully employing tight and overlapping patterns. When recoveries are made, you'll have some added difficulty in identifying the particular period from which they originated, especially if the home was occupied for numerous generations, and STYLE DRIFT in certain common household items will quickly become apparent...a deep signal may produce a two-tined fork from the earliest period of occupation, while a shallow signal may produce a silver plated fork with four tines lost or discarded at a more recent date. Style drift in buttons will be equally as obvious as you proceed from early one-piece metal buttons of brass, pewter, tombac, or copper, to later two-piece buttons. At one particular home site I worked in the past, I remember recovering several colonial buttons, a War of 1812 button from the 2nd Artillery, and a state militia button from the period of the Civil War, all from the same side of a cellar hole.

Early home sites, which were used over a long period of time, allow us to see the progress and some of the technological advances that have been made over those intervening years.

Lost Villages And Ghost Towns

When we usually think of a "ghost town", the immediate image that springs to mind is one of the old West...saloon doors swinging on creaking hinges in a blustery breeze...sagebrush racing down a deserted main street...the eerie sound of loose shutters flapping against window casements and the once boisterous carousing of miners on a Friday night is now only the shadow of a whisper carried on a distant wind.

However, ghost towns and lost villages are not confined to the West..they are found in the East on a regular basis. When a new turnpike was constructed, or a rail line laid out, whole communities often resettled. When natural resources were depleted, or no longer needed in light of newer technological advances, entire towns were abandoned.

I know of two such abandoned villages within fifty miles of where I live. One village was abandoned within the first quarter of the 1800s, and the coins, buttons and relics recovered from the site provide us with a view of the period between 1785 and 1820. Of the dozens of coins recovered on the site, none are more recently dated than 1812, while the earliest date from the Revolutionary War era. The majority of dwellings on this site were log cabins and evidence of cellar holes can only be found in two instances.

Bell, buttons, and "buzzer" surround brass spigots recovered on the site of a "lost village". The two-holed "buzzer" was formed from a worn colonial coin.

Most of the area once occupied by this village is covered with hay fields, and clues that might be read on the surface of a freshly plowed corn field were obscured by the growing grasses. In our attempts to find where the individual cabins were located, we worked all the high crests of the surrounding hills with our discrimination on a very low setting...often times, we ran our detectors in ALL METAL MODE...we were looking for nails that may have been used in the construction of the cabins. Once we found areas with high concentrations of nails, we boosted our discrimination levels to block small ferrous targets and began running tight patterns over the area. The resulting searches of each log cabin site provided us with numerous coins, buttons and other artifacts from that period of time.

In the case of the other abandoned village, the remains can now be found in the depths of a heavily wooded area. Walking down the now silent roadways that crisscross between dozens of cellar holes gives one an eerie feeling. The site has produced hundreds of coins dating from the late 1700s to the 1890s. Washington inaugural buttons, shako plates from the War of 1812, handfuls of buttons covering all periods and wars have been found. The site is literally a cornucopia of American history waiting to be uncovered. Of special consideration, is the fact that the site can be worked during most seasons of the year and it makes a fantastic "back-up" site when we are unable to get into the fields.

When doing the research for surrounding areas, be sure to note any communities that were abandoned or moved, as the sites on which they were once located offer the relic hunter a "time capsule" to the past.

Chapter 9

Laws And The Relic Hunter

Relic hunters must be acutely aware of the laws governing our activities. I have made an earlier mention about staying away from all FEDERAL lands with your detector. This was not a casual warning, and don't expect any federal authorities, National Park Service agents or U. S. Attorneys, to believe the fact that you strayed onto national park lands by accident. Accidentally, or not...unwittingly, or not...it will make no difference. You will be prosecuted under the Archaeological Resources Protection Act of 1979, commonly known as ARPA.

This act was passed into law to protect archaeological resources on federal and Indian lands...HOWEVER, we have recently seen a few incidents where the act is being applied to PRIVATE property as well. How the law is interpreted is very important for the relic hunter to understand.

In the Archaeological Resources Protection Act, Section 3 defines exactly what an ARCHAEOLOGICAL RESOURCE is: "The term 'archaeological resource' means any material remains of past human life or activities which are of archaeological interest, as determined under uniform regulations promulgated pursuant to this Act. Such regulations containing such determination shall include, but not be limited to: pottery, basketry, bottles, weapons, weapon projectiles, tools, structures or portions of structures, pit houses, rock paintings, rock carvings, intaglios, graves, human skeletal material, or any portion or piece of the foregoing items. Nonfossilized and fossilized paleontological specimens, or any portion or piece thereof, shall not be considered archaeological resources, under the regulation under this paragraph, unless found in an archaeological context. No item shall be treated as an archaeological resource under regulations under this paragraph unless such item is at least 100 years of age."

Most of the relic hunters I know would hate to spend an entire day in the field digging up items that were LESS than one hundred years old, so I guess the government would consider the majority of our finds as archaeological resources. However, since these finds are being recovered on PRIVATE property and not federal property or Indian lands, it is not a violation and not prosecutable...USUALLY.

Relic hunting or collecting of artifacts has suddenly become a prosecutable offense through an overly generous interpretation of Section 6, subsection (c), which states: "No person may sell, purchase, or exchange, in interstate or foreign commerce, any archaeological resource excavated, removed, sold, purchased, exchanged, transported, or received in violation of any provision, rule, regulation, ordinance, or permit in effect under State or local law."

What does it mean? Let's illustrate the problem and interpretation with an example of how you could be prosecuted under the Archaeological Resource Protection Act of 1979.

For whatever reason, you have failed to get permission to search a site. You dig up a Minie ball, fired during a Civil War skirmish, in a farmer's field. The farmer sees you in his field, calls the police, and files charges of trespassing against you. The police confiscate the Minie ball as part of the evidence. Since they can't prosecute you for "felony stupidity" for your failing to get permission, you decide to plead guilty to the charge of trespassing and pay a small fine. You realize full well the error of your ways and apologize to the court and the landowner for your oversight. However, you have been found guilty of breaking a local ordinance. In a "worst case scenario," you can still be prosecuted under the ARPA, through Section 6, subsection (c), if your mistake has been noted by an overzealous U. S. Attorney.

If you are prosecuted and convicted of being in violation of subsection (c), subsection (d) sets the limits on how severely you could be penalized: "Any person who knowingly violates, or counsels, procures, solicits, or employs any other person to violate, any prohibition contained in subsection (a), (b), or (c) of this section shall, upon conviction, be fined not more than $10,000 or imprisoned not more than one year, or both." When the ARPA was amendend and strengthened in 1988, the dollar amount representing a FELONY was reduced from $5,000 to $500 and some of the wording was changed to include "attempts" to damage archaeological resources.

Recently, during a discussion with a chief ranger of the National Park Service, a few other "interesting" developments came to light. Included within that $500 dollar limit is the cost per hour for a professional archaeologist of their choice, his traveling time, the cost of his transportation and meals, and I am sure an additional number of "tack ons" that have yet to be devised. In a recent case, the digging of two musketballs from the bottom of a dried out swamp gave a "damage" estimate in excess of five hundred dollars! I think we can all get the picture here...under ARPA, there really isn't any misdemeanor charge if the government wants to pursue a relic hunter for a felony. Their ways may seem somewhat less than artful, but they can be highly effective!

However, we are assuming that the Minie ball and any damage done to the farmer's field was under five hundred dollars. If a determination is made that the site damage and value of the "archaeological resource" is greater than five hundred dollars, you could face double the fine and time. We're not done with this case, however. Remember, this is THE WORST CASE SCENARIO.

In Section 8, subsection (b), REWARDS; FORFEITURE, "All archaeological resources with respect to which a violation of subsection (a), (b), or (c) of section 6 occurred and which are in the possession of any person, and all vehicles and equipment of any person which were used in connection with such violation may be (in the discretion of the court or administrative law judge, as the case may be) subject to forfeiture to the United States." This subsection continues on, but the picture isn't any brighter down the road...you won't be going down the road, as your car or truck will be sold at government auction...YOU'LL BE UP THE CREEK WITHOUT THE PROVERBIAL PADDLE! If, per-chance, you were able to get your vehicle back after a long and protracted legal defense, the courts can order you to pay a storage charge which could possibly total an amount greater than the value of the vehicle. Either way, the creek looks pretty dismal!

Various state and Federal agencies protect historic sites. Using a metal detector on such grounds is not only illegal, but can result in stiff fines and possibly jail. Be sure of where you are and ALWAYS seek permission before attempting to relic hunt a site.

In Section 12, SAVINGS PROVISIONS, subsection (c), it states that, "Nothing in this Act shall be construed to affect any land other than public land or Indian land or to affect the lawful recovery, collection, or sale of archaeological resources from land other than public land or Indian land." That means that private land is exempt as long as there are no violations of state or local laws.

It is of the utmost importance that you protect yourself by knowing how laws governing relic hunting apply. Each state has its own unique set of laws. Don't just read the laws of the states in which you relic hunt...STUDY THEM. Call the "parks and recreation" department at your state capitol and have them send you a packet of regulations concerning their historic preservation laws. These will usually be available to you free of charge.

A handy and instrumental little booklet entitled FEDERAL HISTORIC PRESERVATION LAWS is available through the U.S. Government Printing Office, Superintendent of Documents Mail Stop:SSOP, Washington, D. C. 20402-9328.

One of the best guides I have seen on the market dealing with the laws facing anyone desiring to use a metal detector on public lands is TREASURE LAWS OF THE UNITED STATES compiled by R. W. "Doc" Grim. Included within the covers of this inexpensive text are copies of Federal laws concerning historic preservation, along with laws and addresses of contacts for each state. In the initial pages of the book actual ARPA cases are cited along with a highly interesting section entitled, "Legal Backgrounds of Archeological Resources Protection." If you don't already have a copy of this book, I would consider it a wise investment for any future relic hunter.

The key factor has always been, and will always be, getting permission to search a property that has been revealed in your research. Searching property WITHOUT permission places the individual relic hunter in the untenable position of being liable to prosecution. Knowing how the system works, knowing the laws that regulate our activities, and where we are allowed to hunt, should always be among the primary concerns of all relic hunters!

Chapter 10

Exciting Hunts & Interesting Finds

Whenever conversations turn to the field of relic hunting, a few questions are sure to arise within the first ten minutes--"What was your best find? Describe your most valuable recovery? Where did your favorite hunt take place?"

On the surface these might appear to be easy questions to answer, but they are not, and I've spent many hours attempting to isolate and distill the ingredients of numerous hunts and various recoveries to come up with a satisfactory answer.

I'd probably have a good deal more success coming up with an answer to the question, "What was your worst hunt?" Believe me, there have been more than a handful of that variety which will forever stick in my mind. Those particular hunts were usually conducted with inadequate preparation and faulty research. Sometimes, especially when you are dealing with little known sites, the documentation is scarce and full of holes. The relic hunter is forced to continue his pursuits with a "gut instinct" and playing hunches. If laboring under such handicaps, the success rate approaches fifty percent, consider yourself lucky. The relic hunter is often forced to work with sub-standard research tools at his disposal, but it is perseverance, the ability to "stick to it", and the time consuming re-evaluation of research in the light of failure, which can often produce the desired results.

I have been on other hunts that could kindly be termed "less than remarkable"---hunts based on solid research and standing excellent chances of meeting success, but which have been doomed to failure by the passage of time...a section of farmland that once contained a Revolutionary War era headquarters and hospital which was recently purchased by the Federal government and is now off limits...a French and Indian War fort complete with an excellent view of a lake, its remains now covered by a hotel complex...the site of a colonial tavern destroyed by the placement of an expressway...the remains of a fort dating from King George's War paved over by a supermarket parking lot. Research had enabled me to locate and pinpoint each of these sites, but it was "PROGRESS" which defeated the recovery of information and relics.

Some hunts have been thoroughly exciting, not from the viewpoint of recovered relics, but from being placed in dangerous situations while on the quest---sudden summer storms encountered while returning from a site in a canoe, the white-capped waves crashing over the bow and threatening to capsize us--- encounters with bears and poisonous snakes in the deep woods--- the careless stepping on a loose stone and the resulting slide toward the edge of a cliff---all images firmly fixed in my mind of exciting hunts...images of which I scarcely enjoy being reminded!

In reality, the type of hunts I've so far mentioned---the failures and "white-knuckled" experiences---have been in the minority, and the truly fantastic experiences I have been fortunate enough to enjoy over nearly twenty years of relic hunting are numerous.

This book, so far, has given you the "how-to" basics of research and relic hunting techniques so that you might, on a first-hand basis, experience the thrill of recovery. I've also tried to illustrate and illuminate some of the procedures that can and should be completed following those recoveries, so the "story" behind your relics will not be lost...so that valuable information along with your relics will be preserved. I've also attempted, in some small way, to bring you along on a typical hunt to our "colonial era fort" to give you an idea of how many relic hunts are conducted and to briefly mention some of the things you might expect to find. However, while it is difficult to answer some of the questions with which this section of the book began, I can surely weave a few tales of great hunts and finds I've encountered over the years.

Let's leave the "how-to's" behind us and enter the realm of THE RELIC HUNTER...the only passports you need to embark on this adventure are your detector, your determination, and your desire. We will walk along the overgrown trails of time...back to a simpler world, a time in which men lived by their wits, or died for lack of them...back to a time that witnessed the birth of great nations born in the crucible of war and hammered into shape by the movement of armies...back to a time when "giants" walked the earth and men of iron and grit were the standard, rather than the exception...a time of statesmen, rather than politicians, a time of hot lead and cold steel, rather than plastic. Yes, there once was such a time...it's mostly gone now, but it is the job and passion of the relic hunter to seek out the clues and evidence of those heroic eras.

Bombs, Bullets and Balls

As usually is the case, dawn found us enroute to the site. The cabin of the car was filled with the scent of freshly brewed coffee and the talk was relics---batteries were fully charged and so were our hopes for a successful hunt on the battlefield.

The first hints of day came slowly and a thick fog hung over the site adjoining the river. We were greeted by an assembly of crows from the woodline as we trekked across the acres of newly harvested corn. We were walking on historic grounds, watered centuries ago by the blood of heroes, and a sense of timelessness enveloped us, ushering us into the time that WAS rather than the time that IS.

It would not have unduly surprised me to hear a distant tattoo on a drum or the shrill notes of a fife pierce the fog...cannon fire would have been at home on this site and the sound of coarse, quick orders wouldn't have been far out of place Such things ran through my mind as I rested my pack against the thick trunk of an ancient oak, and began preparing my detector for the hunt.

A visual survey, in this case, would have been of little use and the order of the day was to begin running loose patterns until the first relic of the battle was brought to light. Somewhere on those fields a bloody contest had been fought centuries earlier...the tide of battle surging first one way, then the other, during several hours of combat. As we began running our patterns over the soft ground and through the thick fog, we knew the evidence of that battle would be hard to mistake.

As I bent over my third or fourth plug, my hopes were running high...the target signal was in the musketball range and I was not disappointed when I pulled that small piece of slightly flattened lead from the base of a cornstalk. I immediately relayed the information to my partner, and it was only minutes before he had recovered one, as well. As part of our strategy, we had earlier decided to mark each relic recovery. Small surface stones were used to accomplish this task, and by the time the sun had dissipated the fog, we were able to look back on a number of these "mini-cairns". From the recovery pattern displayed behind us, it was easy to note that the frequency of good finds were increasing as we continued to search into the "hot spot" of the field. The fact that the recovery pouch on my hip was getting noticeably heavier was another good indicator that our research had been on target.

Curved iron fragments began to be mixed with the musketball recoveries and after a quick field cleaning they were easily identified as mortar bomb fragments. After recovering over a half dozen of these, it was time to head back to the pack and empty my recoveries. In addition to musketballs and mortar fragments, my partner had also recovered a few vented pewter buttons, good evidence that our recoveries dated from the French and Indian War.

Battlefield recoveries often come in amazing varieties and quantities. We were able to recover, during the course of our hunt, hundreds of musketballs and numerous mortar bomb fragments.

Like all successful hunts, the hours that day flew by. We backtracked parallel to our initial run, duplicating the quantity and variety of finds. We continued working these parallel patterns for hours before deciding to extend our hunt further into the field. While the frequency of the musketballs began to drop off, there was a noticeable increase in the number of mortar fragments...it was then that the first really large and broad signal was noted. I had my hopes up, but I tried to guard them. I could almost feel the target beckoning and flirting with me. I knew what I wanted it to be...knew how much I wanted the afternoon portion of the hunt to begin with such a recovery, but I didn't give voice to it for fear of ruining what had already been a day of incredible recoveries.

Opting for my entrenching tool, I began to dig on the signal. Thinking about pinpointing was useless as the signal spread over the surface for a solid two feet. As I dug, I noticed the rusty discoloration of the ground and once again my hopes began to surge. To say that my pulse had slightly quickened would have been the understatement of the century!

I suddenly heard the edge of my entrenching tool hit the edge of something, giving a slight metallic sound. I probed with the tip of my small digger and located the target and began clearing away the loose soil from the upper surface. The top of a rusty ball emerged from beneath the soil, and I simply sat back and looked at it for a couple of minutes. I signaled to my partner and he sensed that something interesting had just been uncovered. He hurried over...and then we BOTH stood looking at it for awhile before removing it from the ground.

That was the first of five cannonballs we were able to recover from the field and it was the first cannonball of the season. Over a hundred fifty musketballs, twenty-five pounds of mortar bomb fragments, and an assortment of buttons and buckle fragments were recovered during the course of that first hunt on the site. There have been quite a few return trips to the site, especially in the spring when the ground has been turned, and while the frequency of the finds of that first day were never duplicated, the memories of that initial hunt...the THRILL of that initial hunt, will forever be in my mind!

"The Island"

Awash in a sea of growing corn, it gave the complete illusion of being an island...the rock-bound borders and the stand of tall trees did little to diminish this resemblance, but only tended to enhance it.

Viewed from the top of an overlook and compared with our maps, we knew we were looking at a potentially untouched site. Other than the asphalt and a few additional secondary roads, the routes along the point of land matched almost perfectly with those originally laid out during the 1750s.

Permission was readily granted by a local dairy farmer and following the establishing of our camp at the border of a nearby lake, we returned to the "island" to try our luck.

The "Island", standing in the sea of corn, was an undiscovered relic site dating from the French and Indian War period. Numerous interesting finds were made on its "shores".

There's something about walking down a farm road with the gently blowing breezes rustling through the cornstalks...it's hard to put your finger on just what IT is, but it seems like music to the ears of the relic hunter when he knows the magical moments of recovery may be just around the next corner.

We placed our packs at the base of a large tree, and after adjusting our detectors, set out in opposite directions to begin the search. Within ten minutes, the first recovery was made, and while it was small and somewhat obscure, it was nonetheless an important indicator for a French and Indian War site.

Whether it was due to the lack of small shot cavities of some gang-molds during that period, or to combat the boredom on isolated frontier posts, it was very common on sites dating from the French and Indian War to find cut musketballs...musketballs not simply sliced in half, but diced into quarters and eighths. As I held it between my fingers, I sensed that we were only minutes away from the next important recovery.

The next relic that met the light of that mid-summer day confirmed my suspicion that we had found an untouched site. As my partner called to me through the dense brush to identify the object he had just unearthed, I imagined a pretty standard item for this type of site, but I was amazed when I saw him holding a fascine knife in the air. The wooden handle had long ago rotted away, but the rest of the tool, covered with a layer of light rust, was still solid and its blade, still sharp enough to render good service after more than two centuries in the ground.

A very small sampling of some relics recovered on the "island" includes musketballs, buckle fragments, pewter buttons, coat weights, and a brass belt tip.

The first two day hunt on the "island" rewarded us with a number of interesting relics, and on subsequent hunts—hunts where we had to listen a little deeper and play every card we had...use every skill and detecting trick at our command...the frequency of recoveries may have become progressively less, but when we camp in that lake-side area, the "island" is still the spot we always visit first. Like pilgrims to an ancient shrine we are always drawn to its shores with the hope that we may have missed something significant, but even more than that hope, it seems the RIGHT way to begin any major hunt in that region. The island is a generous lady and she always yields one last treasure on each of those visits.

There is a lingering peacefulness on the island and the memories of the wind in the cornstalks is the remembered music that eases the passage of those long winter nights of research.

Brown Bess And Bayonets

Gun parts are among the most numerous finds relic hunters uncover—and whether you are searching a battlefield or skirmish site where these weapons were used for defense—or a colonial homesite where the flintlock was used as a primary tool for putting meat on the table, you're sure to run across a number of these interesting relics during your searches.

The day of the hunt was one of but a long series of hot and dry summer days. Radio stations were reporting a drought and from the way the site looked at our arrival, you'd have believed it. The small stream that had once ran through the center of the site had been reduced to a trickle and the area that was once a shallow swamp was empty of water, exposing a thick layer of mud and rotting organic debris. When we had begun working the site, months earlier, I could quickly tell that it had been "hammered" by legions of relic hunters in the past.

Using some of the skills I've detailed earlier concerning this type of site, I was able to pull just enough from the depths of the ground to "tease" me into repeated return visits. Yet, despite the series of teases, I knew there was something about the site which kept luring me back...something still unfound...some guarded secrets lingering in the depths of the soil!

On that particular hunt day, I ranged out farther from where I would normally have begun my search, and began working the thick area of ferns growing on the borders of the swamp. My boots were working double-time flattening the ferns to allow for a close coil sweep over the surface of the ground.

The first recovery was a musketball, but strangely enough, it resembled a large acorn as the ball had a small amount of rotted wood surrounding its base. This puzzled me at first, but fifteen minutes later, I detected what appeared to be a small piece of rotted wood. On picking it from the loose earth, I immediately noted its excessive weight. Trapped within the cocoon of wood was what I assumed was a musketball—an assumption which later in the week proved correct when the tree fragment was X-rayed.

I continued my search to the edge of the swamp, and then INTO it, my boots sinking about three inches into the mud as I resumed my search patterns. I knew this was probably going to be my last search on the site and I didn't want to leave any stone unturned. Besides, I knew that I would probably never again see the swamp that dry. It was going to be my last and best shot.

While working my search patterns toward the opposite side of the swamp, I received my first large signal. After pinpointing, I dug into the reeking mud. At about eight inches a clump of mud was pulled from the bottom of the hole, and sitting on top of the pile were two whitened musketballs. Sweeping the coil over the hole, it was easy to see that my recovery work had just begun.

Looking into the depths of the hole, I saw that it was now half filled with water. After a couple of attempts at using my digging tool with minimal success, I was reduced to rolling up my sleeves and scooping water and mud from the bottom of the hole with my cupped hands. The recoveries continued as I became

Bayonets and tools are frequently found at military encampments. Such large targets cannot hide from today's detectors.

progressively more excited, not to mention more muddied. When the headset finally fell silent, I found that I had recovered a nest of eighteen musketballs, no doubt linked with the loss of a ball pouch over two centuries earlier.

I had little time to speculate on what other relics the swamp might contain as the detector signaled another target only three feet from where the nest had been recovered.

Digging down several inches exposed a rusted iron cylinder poking upright from the bottom of the hole. Suspecting what the relic was, I slid my fingers through the mud and along the cylinder. I hooked my fingers around a curve at the base of the cylinder and gently pulled. Accompanied by the squelching sound of sucking mud, close to a foot and a half of bayonet slid from the depths of the swamp. I held it in my mud encrusted hands and sensed the closeness and magic of those centuries long gone, little realizing I was only minutes away from the best discoveries of the day!

After placing the bayonet in a large zip-lock plastic bag to retain some of the moisture, I headed back to the swamp. It was easy to see from the deep tracks in the mud exactly where I had left off my search patterns, and I jumped back into the mud to pick up the relic trail from where I had left off.

The continued search yielded a couple of pieces of grapeshot, several musketballs, a pewter spoon handle and a button. It was just following the recovery of a musketball that my coil swept over a very large signal about six feet from the edge of the swamp. Digging down, I recovered what first appeared to be a large, heavy, triangular clump of solid mud. Holding it in my hand, I checked the hole and a similar reading raced through my headset. Putting the first target to the side of the hole, I continued the act of recovery until I was holding still another, identical, clump of mud. Protruding from the top of the second piece of mud was a screw which I quickly identified...it was then that all the pieces of the puzzle fell into place—the screw, the roughly triangular shape...I knew what I had found, but only a careful field cleaning of one of the pieces would verify and confirm my suspicions.

Moving to the dry ground on the border of the swamp, I squatted down and removed my Buck knife from its sheath and gently probed and picked away the loose mud from one of the pieces. Slowly the form and contours of the once hidden relic were revealed... with each fragment of falling mud the magic of the past was allowed to shine through. After five minutes of delicate work I found myself holding the complete lock mechanism of a second model Brown Bess musket!

Found in the depths of a swamp, these complete Brown Bess locks were an amazing recovery. When working sites that have been heavily searched, look for those areas that are most difficult to relic hunt...you'll be surprised at what might turn up!

Just WHY two complete and fully serviceable Brown Bess locks had been thrown into the depths of a swamp will always cause me to wonder about the circumstances leading up to that past event. The answers to my questions and speculations will never be answered to my satisfaction, but, as often is the case with relic hunters, we generally find a good deal more QUESTIONS than answers...and running through likely scenarios that fit the unknown facts is part of the ROMANCE that ever follows in the wake of the relic hunter!

Blockhouse Bonanzas

One of my favorite types of relic sites are blockhouses. Often little more than fortified homes, they dotted the colonial land-scape, protecting small villages, fords, bridges, sawmills and fort approaches. The fact that they were large in number is more than offset by the fact that most were usually very small in size, making them difficult to locate. However, once discovered, they offer the relic hunter a highly interesting hunt. Of the many I've hunted, I've yet to be disappointed with the time and energy expended in locating the site when viewed in the light of the recovered relics and the information I've been able to glean from the site. One of these blockhouse adventures stands out from the rest.

It was late spring and just before the planting of crops was to take place in the North Country. A corn stubbled field lay before us and from between those shortened stalks we spied the telltale pile of foundation stones for which we had been searching since the day before.

I pulled the car off the road and onto the field. We unloaded our equipment from the trunk of the car and headed toward the pile of stones a short distance away.

Our initial visual survey turned up several pipe stems, some Cantonware fragments, a French gunflint and the remains of rose-head nails, sure indicators to the age of the site. Placing our packs on the pile of stones, we set out on our search. I was in the process of recovering the first musketball when I caught a glimpse of an elderly man walking in my direction from the farm across the road. I recovered the ball and after placing it in my collecting pouch, I stopped hunting, removed my headset, and offered a "good morn-ing" to our curious spectator who had approached to within a

The remains of a stone-lined well that served the blockhouse. Note the higher growth of vegetation surrounding it . . . always a good indicator for some hidden feature.

couple of yards. His age was reflected in the deep furrows with which the passage of time had laced his face. His eyes were bright, matching a genuine smile as I introduced myself while extending my hand.

"They call me, 'CHRISTMAS'," he said, the smile still firmly fixed on his lips. "It's my name and birthday."

Christmas was a wealth of information about the site having lived beside it for almost half a century, a duration of time which I was thoroughly convinced must be almost half his life. Speaking with him, and hearing the tales of things he had seen turned up by the plow only increased my desire to continue the search. I was torn between the enjoyment of the conversation and the first-hand information I was receiving and the desire to dig. After almost a half hour of steady talk, Christmas wished us good luck, stating something about having to "get the cows out." It was a pleasant intermission in the hunt, but I was happy to get back on the relic hunting trail.

The rows of cut cornstalks provided us with our patterns and I could already see my partners working at making additional recoveries in the distance. I decided to work the area around the blockhouse stones and despite the number of identified iron signals, I was able to pull close to two dozen dropped musketballs from that small area. Later, as I worked out from the foundation remains, the frequency of recovered balls decreased, but I began running into quite a number of colonial buttons of both military and civilian design.

My partners, Dennis and Gene, were having about the same amount of success I was enjoying. Each had recovered iron axe heads from the period, while I had uncovered a small iron pick. Gene followed with a colonial compass case and brass belt tip, and Dennis recovered an ornate knee buckle, its inside brass mechanism still intact and fully functional.

The hours on the site flew by and after dinner that night in camp, under the light of a glowing moon, a roaring fire, and a

Coleman lamp, we examined the recoveries made during the course of the day and set our strategies for the following dawn on the site of the colonial blockhouse. Spread across the table were the reminders of the past in the form of buttons, buckles and balls. We drew a couple of crude maps of the site which would help us employ some of the information given to us by "Christmas" during our short conversation with him.

Blockhouse coin recoveries round out an interesting hunt. Chemicals used in farming have eaten into the coppers, while the Spanish silver remains untouched.

Just after dawn the following day, we were on the site and during the morning portion of the hunt, we were once again joined by our smiling and highly informative elderly visitor. I guess you could say that it was a search to remember and a relic hunting season in which "Christmas" came TWICE!

"ROOKIES"

As I've mentioned earlier, one of the most interesting and rewarding aspects of being a relic hunter is being able to share information and skills...this is especially true when you bring a "rookie" into the field with you and watch as the grip of history suddenly tightens around him. The symptoms of "relic hunting fever" are easily diagnosed and far from subtle. Accompanying this remarkable transformation from coinshooter to relic hunter is the uncanny luck that many "first-timers" experience. I know, I've witnessed it...at times with a certain amount of guarded enyy.

A few examples of such unsurpassed initial good fortune should be enough to illustrate the point that SUCCESS in relic hunting can be accomplished by ANY detectorist once a solid base of research has been established.

<Witness **GENE SALVINO,** one-time avid coinshooter. Any butterfly would be jealous of the metamorphosis Gene under-

went after his first day in the field.

The site we decided to hunt was riddled with the remains of rotten vegetables, but under the surface lay the hidden remnants of a Revolutionary War era fort. Gene initially thought that the site would be a great place to find some very early coins, but that first musketball which witnessed the birth of our nation was enough to push the thoughts of coins into the far recesses of his mind.

During subsequent relic hunts, Gene was able to recover cannonballs and trade axes, buttons and buckles, Spanish silver and colonial tools. His growing library of research and identification books are taking up an ever increasing portion of the available space in his home, while his "field identification" skills are continually being honed to a point where he can usually identify even the most obscure relics within seconds of recovery. Truthfully, I don't think Gene has thought about searching a schoolyard or lawn since we first hooked up together as a team two years ago.

<Witness **DENNIS DAVIDSON**, a relic hunter who came to this portion of the hobby without any experience with a

metal detector. Dennis "cut" his metal detecting "teeth" in the valley cornfields searching French and Indian War sites. The first day in the field, with only the briefest of instructions on how a metal detector should be operated, Dennis was making his first relic recoveries. Since that first hunt he has recovered colonial camp axes, buttons, buckles, and has recaptured his long faded interest in history.

An avid canoeist and an expert behind the paddle, Dennis has guided us to some very remote sites, only accessible by canoe, in our many relic hunts together.

<Witness **ART BRUNNER,** a man with years of experience on the working end of a metal detector. I'd have to give Art the nickname of "Mr. Endurance" as Art usually hits any field with his typical Iron Man Marathon characteristics and demeanor. Good relic finds are never far away when Art is in the field, and while Art continues to work old house sites and farms, it's the relic hunting expeditions to which he most looks forward.

<Witness **ROGER MABEN,** a "returnee" to the hobby of metal detecting, who has sharpened his detecting skills to the point where he threatens to leave little in a field for other team members. The first time Roger accompanied me to a relic site he broke the "century barrier" with a coin from the 1780s...and he's been doing it ever

since! You can never tell what new relic Roger will show up with when he meets the guys down at the river, but it's sure to be a beauty.

<Witness **DOUG JACOMINE,** relative newcomer to the field of relic hunting. Doug amazed us when we met him on a site

just after dawn one morning, producing a Fugio Cent he had recently recovered. Few people know their detector as well as Doug and when he searches a site you can rest assured that nothing is left in his wake...the name "Mr. Precision" would certainly be apt and fitting when it comes to the qualities Doug brings to the field.

There have been numerous other "rookies" I've hunted with over the years and each has left the field with a growing appreciation for our country's rich history...along with representative relic reminders of the times that were in those centuries past. Each has become an amateur historian as they seek the trails and long overgrown paths that weave through the dusty decades.

"The Little Fort On The Hill"

I guess if I ever considered writing a childrens' book on relic hunting this would make a "cute" little title. I could have all kinds of "cute" and thoroughly "cuddly" characters like Carmela Cannonball and Marvin Musket, not to mention gentle Grannie Gunpowder and the sinister Simon Swordedge...however, there was nothing "cute" about this site...it was full of "hot" rocks, thick brush, poison ivy and mosquitoes. It was a "nightmare" in a relic hunter's field of dreams. It had only two things going for it: 1) it was loaded with relics, and 2) it had never been relic hunted. After spending so much time earlier in this book detailing research techniques, I'd sure be happy to tell you I found this site by strictly following my own advice. I CAN'T. Perhaps I should have included a chapter on...right..."DUMB LUCK—HOW IT FINDS YOU!"

There I was, wearing typical relic hunting garb...my bathing suit. A towel draped boldly over my shoulders, cutting a striking (and no doubt DRIPPING) image as I looked at the enframed coin on the wall in the hotel lobby. The caption under the coin stated it was a facsimile of a coin found while excavating the foundation of the hotel. Immediately, I knew the coin was au-thentic. I'd dug far too many of them to know the difference between a copy and the real thing.

I didn't have a detector with me as it was January and the ground was frozen rock solid, but the fact that I could still search for additional remains of the site which might still be in evidence was still a possibility. I quickly changed, threw on a parka and headed out into the parking lot. Rarely do I conduct an on-site visual survey in January, but this was an exciting stroke of good fortune.

With boots firmly planted on the parking lot asphalt, I pivoted around, taking in the surrounding grounds... and THERE IT WAS! It was that simple! I looked at the height of land behind the hotel, saw how it rose above the surrounding hills, how it offered a view of the lake, how it could be easily defended, how its situation offered such a perfect spot for an observation post.

I ascended to the very summit of the hill and walked around attempting to "read" the ground. Surrounding the top of the height was a narrow trench which would have been exactly what I would have expected to find with the remains of a stockaded wall that had long ago rotted away. Examining a woodchuck hole and the earth removed by that industrious animal, I found evidence of black ashes and charred wood. From such scant finds, great images form. I knew I would return with the mid-April thaw and with permission from the hotel owners.

The last week of April found me on the site with detector in hand. The first signal resulted in a vented pewter button with iron shank...inches away a dropped musketball...a foot away, a brass shoe buckle fragment...a yard away, the nib knife from a colonial inkwell set...a flint still held in its lead wrapper...a 1738 King George copper (a facsimile? RIGHT!)... an ornate knee buckle...a pewter cuff button from the British 47th Regiment! The list of relics could go on and on for pages.

By the end of the first day of relic hunting, I had recovered over thirty buttons of various sizes, and designs, several sleeve links, dozens of dropped musketballs, and more than a half dozen coins of the period, dating from the 1690s through the 1730s. On the second day, I again worked the summit, but I also encountered numerous finds while searching the adjoining slopes.

In hunts during the following years, with new strategies and new advances in metal detecting technologies, the site still produces a handful of interesting relics with each visit.

The site was a fluke, but it wasn't the last time I was turned onto a great relic hunting area by something that bordered on coincidence. Don't wait for "dumb luck" to find you—in fact, this might be a good time to re-read the section on RESEARCH—but, you can expect to find that variety of luck when you LEAST expect it. Listen, be observant, and remember the story about

To this day, the "little fort on the hill" continues to produce interesting relics for any relic hunter willing to work slowly and listen deep.

"The Little Fort on the Hill"...sometimes it just happens that way!

Kings - Spanish And Otherwise

There can be no more sure an indicator to the age of a site than a coin from the period. Such coins are a BONUS for the relic hunter and are rather coincidental to the other relics for which he is searching. But, being termed "coincidental" should imply, in no way, that they are anything less than exciting when recovered!

Over the years, I've been able to recover well over a hundred coins dating from the 1700s, and I've yet to find myself saying, " Gee, just ANOTHER King George copper."

Depending on the type of site the relic hunter finds himself searching, the quality of the recovered coins will vary. On sites that have seen the constant seasonal turning of the soil, accompanied by a variety of applied chemicals used in the farming process, the coins will be of minimal numismatic value, unless, of course, they happen to be made of silver or gold. Being able to read a date on a copper coin found under the described circumstances should be considered the exception, rather than the rule, and determining the type of coin is often reduced to the ability of being able to note in which direction the head of the king is facing or a couple of barely visible letters surrounding the profile. In many cases, the experienced relic hunter will appear to be almost "psychic" when asked to identify a coin presented to him by a novice after a recovery has been made in the field.

In cases where recoveries have been made in the deep woods, places where the ground has never been turned and treated with chemicals, the coins are generally of high quality and easily identified. Coins recovered under these circumstances only bear the wear of circulation, and the dates and inscriptions are generally strong and bold.

Single coin recoveries are the general rule, however there

have been several fortuitous occasions where I have been able to make multiple coin recoveries, and two such hunts are permanently etched in my mind.

British coppers are the most common coins found on colonial sites. When found in unturned soil they can be recovered in a remarkable state of preservation!

In the first case, we could not have asked for a LESS auspicious beginning for a relic hunt. The day was in mid-November and from the looks of the sky we felt the hopes of seeing any burst of sunlight would be slim. Within the first two hours, we rapidly saw our chances for success diminish. We were in the process of working a rocky slope and almost simultaneously we had equipment failures. While attempting to dislodge a large stone which was covering a target, my partner used a little too much power on the end of his entrenching tool and snapped the handle in half.

Minutes later, as I was in the process of pinpointing a target on the upper levels of the slope, I felt my headset being ripped from my head. I turned quickly and was able to witness the extraordinary sight of nearly a thousand dollars worth of detecting equipment rolling down the rocky face of the slope...I never realized the incredible BOUNCING capabilities incorporated in the engineering and manufacturing of high-tech electronic equipment as I watched my detector and headset leaping over large rocks before coming to rest against the base of a huge tree over a hundred feet below me. Obviously, the first thoughts and words that came to my lips are unprintable.

After scrambling down the slope, I viewed the damage. The lower pole assembly was broken, and the lower half of the pole and my coil were four feet away, stretching the limits of the coil cable. The dents and scratches on the metal housing of the detector were a grim reminder of the acrobatics I had witnessed seconds earlier. The meter plastic was shattered, the tuning knob was gone, and the headset wire was almost completely pulled from the plug. My second set of comments were no more printable or pleasant than the first.

With my detector "down" and my partner's digging tool totally unfunctional, we decided to team-up and continue with the hunt. Amid a snow squall that had just developed, we returned to the upper slope and recovered my target before heading to the relatively flat surface above the slope. While one of us used the detector, the other dug, and in this fashion we were able to recover several dozen musketballs and a few buttons during the course of the next two hours.

It was while working the very rim of the slope when the detector signaled a target at the edge of a large, flat rock. The target was a colonial button, and as I check the hole again, I found that the edge of the rock also seemed to be producing a signal. We dug under the rock and produced a King George copper dated 1735. Running the coil over the top of the rock produced a series of faint signals. It took both of us to dislodge the rock and send it crashing down the slope, but when we passed the coil over the exposed ground, we knew that our efforts had been worthwhile.

Pinpointing individual targets was almost impossible as there were so many signals. We were able to recover two more colonial buttons and another dozen coppers dating from the period of King William, King George, and George II. One of the factors that had made the pinpointing so difficult, was the fact that all these targets had been mixed with dozens of various sized FISHOOKS from the period of the French and Indian War. At some time, centuries past, it appeared that someone had lost his "possibles" bag and during the course of that time, under the influence of weather and gravity, the large flat stone had slid over the remains. We carefully noted all the recoveries when we split up the finds later that evening, and each of us were able to retain relic reminders of that incredible hunt!

Spanish silver finds are relatively frequent occurrences in the field when searching colonial sites, and the sight of a one real, sitting in the bottom of a freshly dug hole is something which is always welcomed.

Generally, the most common field recoveries are in the form of medios, or half reals, and one real pieces - but, there are those other occasions when Spanish silver of larger denominations come from the earth, and one of my favorite and most exciting multiple finds was locating a "glory hole" of Spanish silver from the mid-1750s!

Each previous visit to the recovery site had produced quantities of musketballs and buttons, and it was a rare hunt when either my partner or myself didn't leave the field with a cannonball in our packs.

We always selected the same base camp for our equipment, knowing that a familiar spot in the deep woods would save us time when we needed to relocate our packs, and it seemed we usually ranged a good distance from our packs before putting our detectors into operation. However, on the day of that well remembered hunt, I decided to start running my search patterns from the area of our packs and head in a different direction.

I noticed two small knolls to my right and decided to run my search pattern in the cleft between them. The brush was sparse and it was easy to cover most of the ground with the sweep of my search coil. I stopped at the base of one knoll to recover a couple of fired musketballs, and as I began working my way through the cut, another strong signal ran through my headset.

I cut a large plug in the dry forest floor and put it to one side. I checked the hole and noted that it still contained the target. I ran my hand through the loose soil and suddenly, five silver "cartwheels" were revealed! I didn't stop to check for dates or quality, but scooped them up in my hands, noting only that they were SPANISH PIECES OF EIGHT! I was astonished, and leaving my detector beside the still open hole, I quickly headed out to find my partner.

Few thrills in relic hunting can equal the recovery of a Spanish "Piece of Eight" dating from the French and Indian War!

As I passed the coins to my friend for his inspection, I suddenly realized that in my excitement, I had not checked the hole a final time to make sure that no other recoveries remained to be made.

With my partner in tow, I headed back to the recovery site, picked up my detector, and ran the coil over the hole once again. I was thoroughly amazed when the detector began to sing out several more target signals. During the next ten minutes I pinpinted and recovered two small half reals, a one real, and a silver blank, about as big as a nickel. The blank disk was interesting in that it was bent in opposite directions on opposing ends and TEETH MARKS were in evidence on each edge!

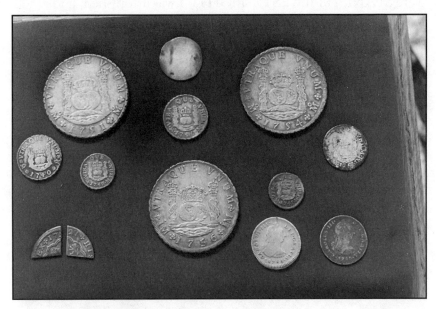

Rarely are British silver pieces found on colonial era sites . . . the Spanish dollar seems to have been the standard of the day.

That memorable recovery was made during the first half hour of the hunt and throughout the course of the succeeding hours, I found myself returning to the area that produced the Pieces of

Eight, in the hopes that I had missed something - and each of the many signals which rang through my headsets was accompanied by the strong belief that more Spanish silver was about to come into the light of day. The fact that no other silver was found that day can never tarnish the excitement that is revisited each time I think about that particular relic hunt!

My Last Great Hunt

Whenever the leaves begin to change color and fall - whenever the first chills are sensed in those October winds as they begin to herald the coming winter, my mind is always drawn toward thoughts of my LAST GREAT HUNT. It has been ten long years since that particular relic hunt, and I would gladly give all of the recoveries I have made during that decade to relive only fifteen minutes of that day.

My kid brother, Dennis, and I hit the site one early fall Sunday morning. The last remains of crop of sweet corn had been harvested the previous month and we set our patterns along the lines running on the exterior of where a colonial fort had once stood. Musketballs were the order of the day, and buttons and coins were a few of the additional bonuses we were able to add to our collecting bags. The DAY was certainly more exceptional than the finds.

The measures of some great hunts are not in the amount of relics that are collected or in astonishing recoveries, but often the gauge is found in the easy conversations and laughter that drift across a campfire as lunch is cooking - often it is found in the amiable camaraderie we share with the friends who hunt with us. These are the unique qualities of any GREAT hunt, and the loss of my brother and hunting partner in 1984, has given me numerous occasions to re-evaluate subsequent relic hunts - and perhaps, it is the PEOPLE we hunt with, and the missions and adventures we share, that is the most memorable and rewarding part of relic hunting.

129

October winds and falling leaves always bring back those fond memories of MY LAST GREAT HUNT - it was very special.

One Final Word - One Final Thought

RELIC HUNTERS - how do we see
ourselves, and the passion that drive us, inexorably, beyond the
realm of schoolyards and parks? Are we to be considered the "bad
boys" of metal detecting because we seek to learn about our history
as a nation on a first-hand basis? - Or perhaps, as it would surely
seem, the target of anyone who shares our passions, but has an
archeology degree hanging on their wall? I don't think there is a
relic hunter who views himself either in that light, or with that
same myopic vision. Let's face it, there are people in the academic
community who do not care for detectorists in general and relic
hunters in particular . . . they never will, for the most part. It is a
rather sad state of affairs when common desires and goals appear to
be on opposite sides of a coin. I know of few relic hunters who
would pass up the opportunity to help archaeologists recover
musketballs and shot from a battlefield. We would relish such a
learning experience and the chance to use our skills to further a
growing understanding of the past. Unfortunately, not many of
these opportunities are ever realized, and instead, we are commonly forced to defend our hobby, interests and passions under
constant and incessant waves of attack from the archaeological
community. Is the quest for knowledge to be outlawed? Is it
desirable to allow plows and chemicals to destroy historic relics
rather than to permit them to be recovered, documented and used
for the purposes of education?

One of our main purposes as relic hunters should not only be
in the collecting of relics and information about a particular
historic period, but in the SHARING of that knowledge with
others. Having been a teacher for well over twenty years, I see

this importance in the questions asked of me by young people
when I use some of my collected relics to illustrate and enhance
discussions and lessons on colonial life or warfare - I can see the
wonder in their eyes as they hold a cannonball used to secure the
country in which they live . . . and sense the awe that being able
to "touch history" brings to their minds.

Making ourselves available to schools and community organi-
zations is something to be encouraged. How much more stimulating and impression-forming it is, to hear, first-hand, about the
recovery of something as simple as a handful of musketballs and
the part they played in a battle, than to view them from the other
side of a glass barrier in a museum!

Most of the sites relic hunters search are of limited archaeological value, and most of the recoveries we make are limited by
the depth of our detectors. We are the savers of the past and not
the plunderers. Our quest for knowledge only differs in the tools
we use. By in large, the sites we hunt would never undergo a
thorough archaeological dig. In the case of a running battle or
skirmish, a place where no structures were involved, what desire
would an archaeologist have in digging up hundreds of acres of
fields? It would be a waste of not only time, but money and archaeological talent. Yes, talent. There are times when only an
archaeologist can interpret the information contained in the
depth of the ground. By the same token, there are certainly a
wealth of times when a skillful detectorist and relic hunter can be
of primary assistance in the recovery of relics.

Along with the growing apprehension relic hunters have
been living with over the last couple of years, has come some
effects the archaeological community may not have considered.
One of these effects has been the loss of record keeping that is so
important to the retaining of knowledge. Written records have
been destroyed or are no longer kept, and sites, once so freely
relayed to the archaeological community, are guardedly kept
secret. This is the worst possible situation for all members con-

cerned. The current state of affairs will only continue to deterio-
rate until some type of coalition between relic hunters and archaeologists can be established . . . a coalition based on common
understanding and respect for the skills each side possesses. If half
the energy wasted arguing between groups was spent in finding a
common ground and a peaceful and intelligent accord . . . if the
money spent by the Federal government on prosecutions were
given for the use of educating relic hunters and detectorists on
proper recovery and documenting techniques, our nation's history
can and would be preserved for all generations to come. Oh well,
we can hope.

I guess to be a relic hunter you also have to be a little naive,
an eternal optimist and an incurable romantic . . . GUILTY AS
CHARGED!

Relic Hunter - the book

About the Author - - - -

For nearly two decades, readers of treasure hunting magazines have enjoyed the adventures **Ed Fedory** has taken them on with his writing and relic hunting missions. Author of the popular column in *Western and Eastern Treasures*, **"The Relic Hunter"**, and countless metal detecting feature stories, Ed can usually be found on some high peak searching for a colonial observation post, or in a canoe along some weed-choked creek, in a quest to discover a Revolutionary War encampment.

A true outdoorsman, adventurer, and teacher of history, it's Ed Fedory's mission to make history live through his first-hand accounts of recoveries. As Ed says, *"It's a great way to spend a life - - - researching - - - adventuring - - - discovering."*

We'd have to agree!

Notes

Notes

Notes

Notes

Notes

Notes

Notes

Notes

Notes

Notes